# EXPORT CONTROLS

# EXPORT CONTROLS

## Building Reasonable Commercial Ties with Political Adversaries

Edited by
**Michael R. Czinkota**
**In cooperation with Scot Marciel**

**PRAEGER SPECIAL STUDIES • PRAEGER SCIENTIFIC**

New York • Philadelphia • Eastbourne, UK
Toronto • Hong Kong • Tokyo • Sydney

Library of Congress Cataloging in Publication Data
Main entry under title:

Export controls.

Includes index.
1. Export controls--United States.  2. Foreign trade
regulation--United States.  I. Czinkota, Michael R.
II. Marciel, Scot.
KF1987.E86 1984                 343.73'0878    84-4735
ISBN 0-03-071021-9 (alk. paper) 347.303878

Published in 1984 by Praeger Publishers
CBS Educational and Professional Publishing
a Division of CBS Inc.
521 Fifth Avenue, New York, NY 10175 USA

© 1984 by Praeger Publishers

456789 052 987654321

Printed in the United States of America
on acid-free paper

# FOREWORD

It has become increasingly apparent in recent years
that the economic relationship of the United States with the
rest of the world cannot be divorced from its overall foreign policy and security objectives. No longer can our ties
with the Eastern Bloc be solely directed through diplomatic
or foreign policy channels, for the world economy has grown
so integrated that trade with the East represents a significant portion of total U.S. trade. Yet the expansion of our
economic links with the East has not mitigated the foreign
policy and security exigencies inherent in our East-West relations. Instead it has lent compelling significance to
that vital juncture of our commercial relations, foreign policy, and security concerns, prompting the formation and application of export controls.

Underscoring the significance of export controls have
been two important economic trends: the increasing importance of East-West trade to the U.S. economy and the rapid
proliferation of high technology products throughout the
world. On the one hand, American businesses, in the face of
a relatively stagnant domestic economy, have had to turn to
foreign markets, especially the developing economies of the
East, to increase their sales. Concomitantly, the growth of
advanced technology has caused concern among those who realize that some degree of control in technology trade is necessary to protect the security of the West and to promote U.S.
and European foreign policy goals. Many government officials
have defended tighter trade controls as necessary to prevent
Soviet acquisition of militarily relevant technology from
the West. The tension between such concerns and the almost
inexorable demand for increased export trade has made it apparent that the development and implementation of reasonable
East-West export controls represents one of today's greatest
challenges to trade policymakers and the international business executive.

This book focuses on that challenge by assembling the
views of nearly 20 leading experts from the business, legal,

academic, and political communities.  These views, which
were presented in the course of a September 1983 conference
in Washington, D.C. sponsored by the National Center for
Export-Import Studies at Georgetown University, offer en-
lightening perspectives and insights on some of the most
problematic issues arising in East-West relations.

This book constructively contributes to the ongoing,
and vitally important, debate over East-West relations.  The
professionals contributing to this volume, including representatives of the Reagan administration, members of both
houses of Congress, and representatives of law firms, uni-
versities, and businesses, address the wide range of issues
involved in East-West trade and suggest ways that U.S. policy can be improved to better restrict high-technology exports while minimizing the cost to American businesses.

A major strength of this work is that it encompasses
the spectrum of viewpoints, ranging from those advocating
stringent trade controls to those advocating highly liberal
controls.  Furthermore, contributors to the book are all ac-
tively involved in export control issues, either as policymakers, lawyers, business executives, or scholars, providing
the reader with a unique opportunity  to gain an informal
and balanced understanding of these issues.  By presenting
this material in a nonadvocacy manner, the National Center
for Export-Import Studies has again produced an outstanding
source of practical information for policy leaders and business executives about important international trade issues.
The contributions contained in this book are definitely effective in stimulating thought in the direction of the development of a more effective export control policy.  It should
be required reading for anyone concerned with international
trade and with U.S. international economic policy.

Thomas B. Evans, Jr.
Washington, D.C.

# ABOUT THE NATIONAL CENTER FOR EXPORT–IMPORT STUDIES

Most of the contributions to this volume are the result of a symposium in Washington, D.C., sponsored by the National Center for Export–Import Studies (NCEIS) at Georgetown University. The conference was another in a series sponsored by NCEIS in its continuing effort to promote increased communication and understanding among the policy, business, and academic sectors of the international trade community.

NCEIS was established at Georgetown University to provide the in-depth, nonadvocacy research needed by the international trade community and to encourage an international research dialogue among the policy, business, and academic communities. By periodically addressing international trade issues of concern through symposia and publications, the NCEIS outlines near- and long-term research and policy agenda.

NCEIS is also charged with consolidating and expanding the existing body of knowledge on international trade, providing its members in the international trade community with practical services, and speaking with a dispassionate voice for the development of internationally acceptable trade policies. To attain these goals, NCEIS engages in research, communication, advising, and instruction.

# ACKNOWLEDGMENTS

The conference, "Export Controls: Building Reasonable Commercial Ties with Political Adversaries," at which most of the contributions to this volume were presented, was sponsored by the National Center for Export-Import Studies. The NCEIS, however, received generous amounts of help from many individuals. Without their assistance, the conference would not have been the success it turned out to be.

Special thanks are owed to the Honorable Thomas B. Evans, Jr., of O'Connor & Hannan, who assisted in organizing the conference and in inviting many key speakers for the symposium; Dr. Robert Kilmarx of International Analysis Associates, who provided invaluable advice and many suggestions that improved the conference; Ms. Eleanor Lyons Williams of the American International Trade Group, who provided assistance in a variety of ways, devoting a great deal of time to the meeting; Manfred Hamm of The Heritage Foundation, who served as conference program coordinator, and whose work was instrumental in the development of an interesting agenda; last but not least, Mr. Neil Livingstone of Gray & Company, who assisted the center in the development of the conference program and in the overall organization of the meeting.

ix

# CONTENTS

# LIST OF TABLES

# INTRODUCTION

Throughout its history, the United States has been the world's staunchest supporter of the principles of free trade. In the early years following independence, the country's fathers sought to build strong commercial relationships with Britain, France, and the other major powers of Europe, but they were strongly opposed to tying those economic relationships to the political realities that governed the world at that time. On the one hand, the leaders of the United States worked to develop trade ties with Britain, the former adversary, before the deep wounds of the political conflict had healed. On the other hand, John Jay, one of this country's first diplomats, eagerly signed a commercial treaty with friendly France while he opposed France's efforts to develop a political alliance.

Since those early years, American foreign policy has been inextricably linked to the idea of free commerce, during both peace and war. Even during World War I, the United States adamantly opposed both Britain's blockade of Europe and Germany's U-boat attacks against merchant ships. This devotion to the ideal of free trade has been supreme throughout most of U.S. history, but a series of dramatic changes since World War II has forced the United States to compromise its ideals to some extent. To begin with, World War II marked the ascent of the United States to world leadership, and the leaders in Washington no longer could avoid entanglement in the world's political struggles and conflicts. Leaders in the United States have found it impossible to continue to separate economic relationships from political relationships. In addition, the continuing struggle for superiority or equality with the Soviet Union has forced the United States to use its economic power to achieve political objectives.

The second important change since World War II, of course, has been the advent of nuclear weapons and the increasing destructive power of the major countries of the world. This increasing destructive power, centered especially

xvii

in the two superpowers, has made the idea of war so horrify-
ing that nations are loath to use their military power to
achieve political goals. Given this reality, the United
States--along with many other countries--has had to use all
of the other weapons at its disposal, including trade, to
achieve political objectives.

The rise of America to world power, combined with the
need to avoid direct military conflict, has caused the United
States to use trade controls and sanctions. Since World War
II, the United States has developed a major trade control
system, based largely on the use of export controls and trade
sanctions. Export controls have served to limit or delay the
export of items that the government deems to be useful to its
adversaries, and trade sanctions have been imposed to place
pressure on adversary regimes.

Most everyone agrees on the need for export controls,
but the past few decades have seen a major and growing debate
about how best to develop an effective and meaningful trade
control policy. Two changes have made the issue of export
controls more important in recent years: the increasing importance of trade to the U.S. economy and the boom in and
proliferation of technology throughout the world. On the one
hand, American businesses, in the face of a continually stagnant domestic economy, have had to turn to foreign markets
to maintain their share of international trade. This has
led to a growing dependence in the United States on exports,
and business executives have begun to work together to promote proexport legislation in Congress.

The growth in technology, on the other hand, has caused
concern among those who feel that the control of some technology trade is necessary to protect the security of the
West and to promote U.S. and European foreign policy goals.
Many government officials and scholars have defended tighter
trade controls as necessary to prevent Soviet acquisition of
militarily relevant technology from the West.

The inherent dilemma between the economic desire to
export and the national security and foreign policy need to
restrict trade has created an ongoing debate in the United
States about East-West trade. This conflict has been exacerbated by the lack of multilateral cooperation in the
West on trade policy. This lack of cooperation has frus-
trated both business executives--who feel they are losing

markets to foreign firms not affected by export controls—and government officials—who have expended enormous political efforts to restrict the trade of certain items only to see other governments promoting the trade of the very same items.

The debate over export controls reached an apex in late 1983, during the debate over the renewal of the Export Administration Act, the legislation that provides authority for the imposition of trade controls. The debate raged between the Reagan administration, which supports fairly strict controls on trade with the Soviet Union, and business leaders, who generally favor looser restrictions on trade. Members of Congress, who must make the final decision on renewal of the Export Administration Act, were divided in their opinions on the subject.

The conference on which this book is based took place in the middle of this debate over the Export Administration Act and brought together many of the major actors involved in export controls. The debates and discussions of the conference are incorporated in this book, and one will find all of the varying viewpoints presented within its chapters.

Because much of the debate on export controls revolves around the Export Administration Act, much of the discussion in the book concerns this legislation. In addition, the book provides both a theoretical examination of trade sanctions and controls and an analysis of the effects of trade controls on individual companies. By presenting a wide variety of viewpoints on the subject, this book should enable readers to form their own opinions on the important issue of export controls.

# I
# THE USE OF
# TRADE  CONTROLS

Part I consists of five contributions and serves to
lay the groundwork for the book's discussion of U.S. export
control policy. Part I begins with some discussion of the
theoretical and historical use of trade controls and then
gradually shifts to an examination of the development of U.S.
trade control policy. The first two chapters provide a historical and theoretical background on export controls and
trade sanctions, and the following three chapters examine
current U.S. policy in light of historical experience.

Michael R. Czinkota examines the use of trade controls
and sanctions, focusing on the reasons for the imposition of
controls. After giving a summary of the basis for the use
of sanctions, Dr. Czinkota develops a taxonomy of trade controls and examines the problems inherent in trying to classify such controls. He concludes by noting that trade controls,
while rarely successful, sometimes may be better than some
of the alternative policies.

Gary Clyde Hufbauer and Jeffrey J. Schott analyze the
historical use of economic sanctions as a tool of foreign
policy. They present a table summarizing 99 instances in
which trade sanctions have been used since 1914 and argue
that such sanctions were rarely successful in accomplishing
their goals. Rather than ending with this conclusion, the
authors delve deeper into the use of economic sanctions, arguing that the rate of success when using such sanctions may
depend on the countries involved and on the goals of the
country imposing the sanctions.

Richard F. Kaufman's chapter provides a fine transi-
tion between the historical emphasis of the first two chapters and the more current emphasis of the final two chapters
of the section. Kaufman tries to set the framework for the
discussion of U.S. policy by examining some of the very broad
questions of East-West trade. He argues that the crucial
question is how to develop an East-West trade policy that
bears a logical relationship to U.S. strategy toward the
Soviet Union. Then, after examining the history of U.S.

1

trade control policy since World War II, he argues that current U.S. policy suggests the lack of a cohesive, well-thought-out policy that fits into an overall strategy toward the Soviet Union.

In his remarks, Undersecretary of Commerce Lionel Olmer discusses the objectives and goals of current U.S. export control policy. Olmer argues strongly in favor of export controls, especially those controls that delay the transfer of militarily relevant high technology to the Soviet Union. He agrees that such controls cause difficulties, but argues that they are essential to the security of the United States. He also points out the need for controls for foreign policy purposes, noting that they are a useful tool of U.S. diplomacy.

Finally, U.S. Trade Representative William Brock makes a plea for increased cooperation from U.S. allies on trade controls. While claiming that the United States is willing to impose trade controls unilaterally, he argues that multilateral cooperation is necessary to any successful trade policy. Brock examines current U.S. policy and argues that it is a sophisticated policy that differentiates between various socialist countries and works to deal with the problem of cooperation in a constructive manner.

# 1

# INTERNATIONAL ECONOMIC SANCTIONS AND TRADE CONTROLS: A TAXONOMIC ANALYSIS

## Michael R. Czinkota

The use of economic coercion by nations or groups of nations can be traced back as far as the Greek city-states and the Peloponnesian War, or in more modern times, to the Napoleonic Wars, during which the combatants used blockades to achieve their goal of "bringing about commercial ruin and shortage of food by dislocating trade."[1]

The extension of the concept of trade sanctions to that of authorized multilateral enforcement of international rules of conduct is a relatively more recent phenomenon. It is closely associated with the concept of collective security and the prevention of war and was first given formal expression with the establishment of the League of Nations.

Historically, states have used sanctions mostly in preparation for, or conjointly with, war. Due to the increasing global risk associated with war in modern times, however, trade sanctions today are used more and more as isolated actions, quite independent of any considerations of war. This shift in use, combined with the proliferation

AUTHOR'S NOTE: The author appreciates helpful cooperation by Howard Fenton. Jeff Brown assisted in the research.

of trade sanctions, calls for a change in the manner in which analysts view economic warfare.

To understand the use of trade sanctions in modern times, one must understand the basis of and reasons for the sanctions; it is also useful to analyze the background behind the imposition of sanctions, such as the goals of the acting country (or countries) and the method in which the sanctions are imposed. By building a systematic framework of taxonomy that incorporates these variables, one can analyze sanctions in depth to determine their value, and one can assess possible changes in and alternatives to the use of sanctions. The purpose of this chapter is to provide such a framework.

## THE BASIS OF TRADE SANCTIONS

The terms "trade sanctions" and "trade controls" as used here refer to governmental actions that distort free flows of trade in goods, services, or ideas for decidedly adversarial political rather than economic purposes. When conducting an analysis of such economic sanctions, it is useful to begin by examining the auspices and legal justifications under which they are imposed. By understanding the philosophy on which trade control or trade sanction policies are based, the objective of such actions may be seen more clearly. Also, these provisions and their caveats shed light on the probable effectiveness of such actions.

The League of Nations set a precedent for the legal justification for economic sanctions by subscribing to a covenant that provided for penalties or sanctions for breaching its provisions. The members of the League of Nations did not originally intend to use military or economic measures separately, but the success of the blockades of World War I fostered the opinion that "the economic weapon, conceived not as an instrument of war but as a means of peaceful pressure, is the greatest discovery and most precious possession of the League."[2]

In the event of an illegal breach of League provisions, Article 16 of the Covenant directed members "immediately to subject (the violating nation) to the severance of all trade or financial relations. . . ." Succeeding clauses

of the article carried the measures further to provide for
mutual support and, if necessary, force in applying economic sanctions.  It was soon recognized that full application of the article could seriously damage some members,
and the article was subsequently diluted to the point that
compliance was voluntary and no longer automatic.

The idea of the multilateral use of economic sanctions
was again incorporated into international law under the
Charter of the United Nations, but greater emphasis was
placed on the enforcement process.  Article 1 of the
United Nations Charter describes enforcement action as
"effective collective measures for the prevention and removal of threats to the peace and for the suppression of
acts of aggression or other breaches of the peace."  Chapter 7 of the Charter constitutes the counterpart to Article
16 of the Covenant of the League of Nations.  Measures contained in Article 41 of this Charter include "complete or
partial interruption of economic relations and of rail,
sea, air. . . ."

This wording makes enforcement authority much stronger
under the UN Charter than it was under the League Covenant.
While under the diluted interpretation of Article 16 of the
Covenant it had been "the duty of each member to decide
for itself whether a breach of the Covenant has been
committed," the UN Charter gives the Security Council, not
the individual members, the authority to decide what situations require economic sanctions.  Also, sanctions decided
on under Article 41 are mandatory, although each of the
permanent members of the Security Council can veto efforts
to impose sanctions.  The Charter also allows for sanctions
as enforcement action by regional agencies--such as the
Organization of American States, the Arab League, and the
Organization of African Unity--but only with the Security
Council's authorization.

The apparent strength of the United Nations' enforcement system soon revealed flaws.  Stalemates in the Security
Council and vetos by permanent members often lead to a
shift of emphasis to the General Assembly, where sanctions
are not enforceable.  Supervision over regional bodies has
not been exercised.  Also, concepts such as "peace" and
"breach of peace" are seldom perceived in the same context

by all members, and thus no systematic sanctioning policy has developed under the UN.3

As far as U.S. law is concerned, the President has had statutory authority to control trade in times of war or, with the consent of Congress, national emergency, since the enactment of the Trading with the Enemy Act of 1917. But until the end of World War II and the beginning of the Cold War era, the idea of using trade controls during peacetime was unheard of. The decision to exert strict peacetime controls over U.S. exports first manifested itself in the Export Control Act of 1949. The act empowered the President to control the export of "any articles, materials, or supplies, including technical data" in an effort to deny militarily useful exports to the Soviet Union and its allies.

By 1951, it was apparent that foreign availability of controlled items would present a serious obstacle to the success of U.S. policy, and the passage of the Battle Act formally declared the intention of the United States to seek multilateral cooperation. The Coordinating Committee for Multilateral Export Controls (COCOM) was founded and remains a functioning body today as an informal, multilateral organization that attempts to coordinate the national export controls of its member states.

By the early 1960s, pressure from Europe and from parts of the U.S. business community led to a major reevaluation of U.S. export policy. Discussion began to emphasize a proper balance between export promotion and national security, and in 1969, with the introduction of detente, the Export Administration Act was passed to formalize this new emphasis.

Since 1969, the act has been amended repeatedly to accommodate changes in administrative apparatus, foreign availability conditions, and short supply controls, but the distinction made between national security and foreign policy controls in the 1979 amendments is of particular significance. National security controls were to be applied "only when necessary to restrict exports which make a significant contribution to the military potential of another country which would prove detrimental to the national security of the United States." If an item controlled under this provision is available elsewhere, as

determined by the Department of Commerce, its export cannot
be denied unless the President determines that the export
would prove detrimental to the United States.

The 1979 amendments called for foreign policy controls to be used "only when necessary to significantly
further the foreign policy of the United States or to fulfill U.S. international obligations." The President was
given total discretion in deciding whether to apply foreign
policy controls, but he is required to consider alternative
actions and the following criteria before invoking the
controls:

1. The probability that the controls would achieve the intended purpose;
2. The compatibility of the controls with other U.S. foreign policy objectives;
3. The reaction of other countries;
4. The likely impact on the U.S. economy;
5. The ability of the United States to enforce the controls;
6. The foreign policy consequences of not imposing the
   controls.[4]

From this brief review of some of the main legal
bases for economic sanctions, the following summary conclusions can be drawn:

1. Economic sanctions are internationally recognized as
   a legitimate means for preserving international peace;
2. Since peace is a multilateral, rather than a unilateral,
   concern, economic sanctions are of international concern;
3. U.S. sanction policy makes exporting a privilege and
   not a right;[5] and
4. U.S. sanction policy "subordinates sales to strategy"
   to stamp U.S. "goods and technology with a political
   pricetag as well as an economic one."[6]

## BUILDING A TAXONOMY

Having clarified the legal basis for economic sanctions, we can now turn to the development of a taxonomy

for the analysis of trade sanctions. The taxonomy can best
be built by examining the three critical factors involved in
the decision to implement sanctions: the trigger situations
that lead to the imposition; the goals and objectives of
such measures; and the form the imposition of sanctions
takes.

## Trigger Factors

To begin with, one must focus on the conditions or
circumstances that appear to lead to the imposition of
trade sanctions. These "trigger factors" can consist of
direct or indirect threats, be they real or perceived, to
nations. Most directly, economic sanctions can accompany
conditions of war. With the advent of economic nationalism
in the nineteenth century, increased global participation in
trade and investment added a new appeal to sanctions as a
true weapon of war. The Allied blockade of Germany during
World War II was a major expression of this newfound appeal.

Similar but less direct dangers are "threats of war,"
meaning a concrete, tangible threat or expectation of the
outbreak of hostilities, or "threats to national or economic security." The latter two, however, are substantially
more ambiguous and may vary significantly in their definition by each nation or group of nations. This ambiguity is
highlighted by the striking differences of perception
within the United States about U.S.-Soviet trade relations,
where some argue that "all trade with the Soviet Union
carries strategic liabilities,"[7] while others attempt to
differentiate between the direct and the indirect strategic
importance of exports.[8]

All the "trigger factors" discussed thus far involve
direct threats to the nations that seek to impose trade
sanctions. Countries may also invoke economic sanctions
when they are not directly threatened if the conduct or
action of another nation toward third parties is seen to
cause indirect threats to the value systems of politically
powerful factions. Indirect trigger factors leading to
the imposition of sanctions can include broad concerns for
national integrity and collective human rights or more specific concerns, such as individual human rights or environmental considerations.

A final category useful here can be entitled "historic" trigger factors. This category includes military and economic as well as cultural and religious reasons, the origins of which may be shrouded in the mists of time, but which may still be powerful motivating factors leading to the imposition of sanctions. This category is also useful to see the convergence of direct and indirect threats over time.

In reviewing this list of conditions that can lead to trade sanctions, it is interesting to see that these trigger factors differ quite substantially when evaluated on the basis of being necessary and sufficient conditions for economic sanctions. Although the presence of direct threats can easily be seen to provide <u>sufficient</u> reason for the imposition of trade sanctions, this threat presence may also make it <u>necessary</u> to impose the sanction, that is, sanctions should very likely be imposed in direct threat situations. Indirect threats, in turn, may present a <u>sufficient</u> but not <u>necessary</u> condition for imposing sanctions. As a result, the existence of similar, indirect threats may cause different reactions in terms of sanctions. A look at the history of sanction imposition confirms the theory that sanctions will be imposed erratically in response to indirect threats, but it does not confirm the theory that they will be imposed with higher frequency in response to direct threats (with the case of war excluded). Clearly, an analysis of trigger factors is useful but not sufficient to understand fully the use of trade sanctions. It is therefore necessary to analyze and categorize the objectives or goals of countries to gain a better understanding of the reasons for their decision to impose sanctions.

## Objectives of Trade Sanctions

If one had to make some subjective judgments when naming the trigger factors for sanctions, the task becomes even more judgmental when one tries to place into categories the objectives that nations seek to accomplish through the use of sanctions. One cannot easily accomplish such a task using only the objectives publicly stated by the government on imposition of the sanctions because of the frequent multiplicity and ambiguity of the goals stated. In addition, sanctions may be intended for either "short-term or longer-term effects, and objectives may well change over time."[9] The U.S.-imposed gas pipeline sanctions, for example, have been variously justified as being designed to:

1.  protest Soviet responsibility for the declaration of martial law in Poland;
2.  prevent Western European dependence on Soviet gas;
3.  damage, or at least not aid, general Soviet economic development by inhibiting a project of great economic importance;
4.  protest the use of "slave labor" in pipeline construction;
5.  deny the USSR hard-currency earnings from the gas sales in Europe.[10]

At the time of the imposition of economic sanctions, domestic policy considerations and political fervor tend to muddy the waters substantially. In addition, public statements on sanction objectives may be quite different from realistic expectations maintained in a less visible fashion. All this makes suspect the objectives stated by the government when it imposes its sanctions. Unfortunately, evaluating the objectives of the sanctions by analyzing the reasons the government provides for their removal is equally clouded by the domestic and international policy considerations present at that particular time. Although these difficulties reduce one's ability to delineate finely the precise goals of sanctions, some broad categorizations are possible.

Of initial help is Kenneth Abbott's differentiation betwen types of economic sanctions. He suggests a distinction between "instrumental" controls, which are designed to change the behavior of the target country, and "symbolic" controls, through which countries seek simply to communicate some message.[11]

With this as a starting point, the stated major objective of controls (with all the inherent limitations discussed above) can then be used to differentiate further the aims of such measures. The most ambitious is the "total collapse of a country," as was the goal in such massive conflicts as World War II. A second goal which is only

slightly less ambitious could be the "change of government."
In a democratic state, an election could accomplish such a
change, but in a one-party or totalitarian state, a major
political upheaval would be required.  A third possible objective is to achieve a "significant general policy impact,"
while a fourth and final instrumental category would be designed to have a "significant specific policy impact."

Although all four of these categories can be labeled
"instrumental" controls, allowance must also be made for
"pseudo-sanctions" within this general category.  Countries
using the latter type of sanction, which is amply discussed
by Klaus Knorr, set an unrealistically high level of expectations, "pretending to attempt coercion, but actually
serving other ends."[12]  While each of the four instrumental
categories can be a pseudo-sanction, it is difficult to
identify them as such a priori, since high ambitions may
make expectations seem realistic to the sanctioning body,
when, indeed, they are not from an ex posteriori perspective.

Symbolic controls are also difficult to differentiate,
since in most circumstances, nations are unwilling to em-
bark on sanctions with the stated objective of merely sending a message.  The U.S. boycott of the 1980 Olympic Games
in Moscow, in apparent response to the invasion of Afghanistan by the Soviet Union, was an exception and, as such, was
a good example of controls designed to be symbolic rather
than to force the target of the controls to alter its behavior.  Within this general type of sanction, one major
objective may be that of vengeance, reflecting the desire to
seek emotional relief by lashing out at a target.  The goal
is not the effecting of change, but an internal reward,
consumed in the act.[13]  Other alternatives are a "diplomatic protest" and a "strong diplomatic statement."


Manner of Sanction Imposition

A third major factor important for a taxonomy of economic sanctions concerns the way the sanctions are imposed.
Here it is useful to look first at the consensus about
sanctions within the imposing country and second at the same
measure among nations.

Within a nation, the main parties involved in economic sanctions are the policy and business communities and
the individual citizens. The policy community is instrumental in the imposition of control measures and exposes
itself to the risk of public disapproval and the cost of
administering sanctions. The business community is affected
by such actions through lost sales and profits, while individual citizens are exposed to much of the impact, be it
through loss of employment, pleasure (such as travel), or
reward (e.g., Olympic medals).

The desires and fears of each of these groups will,
therefore, be instrumental in determining the extent of
agreement about and support for economic sanctions. Although the burden, costs, and benefits of sanctions will
rarely be distributed equally among all members of all
groups, a consensus about the purpose will lead to a much
greater acceptance of sanctions--even on a voluntary basis.
For example, there was a broad national consensus in the
United States for the sanctions imposed against Iran during the hostage crisis and for some of the critical technology controls imposed against the Soviet bloc countries.
Such a consensus simplifies enforcement of the sanctions
imposed and, therefore, increases their effectiveness. It
does not, however, necessarily contribute to the achieve-
ment of the goals of the sanctions. For example, a consensus about denying critical technology to the Soviet
Union may result in effectively reducing technology flow,
but this fact may not have a significant policy impact on
the Soviet Union. Such a lack of impact may, over time,
result in a weakening of an initially broad consensus,
thus reducing the effectiveness of the sanctions. The U.S.-
imposed grain embargo against the Soviet Union may serve as
an example here. A consensus can best be achieved and maintained if sanctions are imposed in response to widely accepted trigger factors, if the objectives and goals are
clearly understandable and seem obtainable, and if, over
time, some progress is made toward these objectives.

On an international level, sanctions can be imposed
unilaterally or multilaterally. If the goal of sanctions
is "instrumental," and the development of pseudo-sanctions
is not desired, a multilateral consensus is usually necessary to ensure the effectiveness of measures. Such a

consensus, in turn, is determined by the commonality of objectives and the cost of imposing the sanctions. The need
for a commonality of objectives poses, of course, the greatest problem here. Although general objectives, such as the
reduction of threats to peace, can be agreed on relatively
easily, it is the specific objective that results in discord, due to differences in interpretation. At the same
time, general sanctions reduce the willingness for international joint action, while specific sanctions are much more
readily accepted, since they clarify and limit the cost of
such actions.

In this context, it is interesting to observe that the
United States, in its international approach, aims mostly
for specific objectives and general sanctions, an approach
that has "engendered surprise and alarm in the U.S. and
international business communities, anger in allied governments, and extensive legal debate."[14]  Under such circumstances, even if multilateral action is taken, it tends to
be a weak and ineffective gesture, as the case of European
import controls for Soviet products amply highlights.[15]
General sanctions may also result in a gradual build-up of
resentment toward any sanctions, as demonstrated by the
recent statement by West German Foreign Minister Hans-
Dietrich Genscher:  "The break-off of economic relations
anywhere in the world is an unsuitable means to achieve
political goals."[16]

It should be clear that by examining trigger factors,
sanction objectives, and the imposition of sanctions, one
can develop a useful framework for the analysis of trade
sanctions.  This framework, shown in Table 1.1, can then be
used to categorize sanctions retroactively and to interlink
this classification with measures of effectiveness.  Once
such measures are established, the framework can be used in
a prospective manner to determine the potential effectiveness
of future sanctions.


CONCLUSIONS

Although a direct measurement of the effectiveness of
sanctions was not the purpose of this chapter, several con-
cluding comments are offered as policy suggestions and,

TABLE 1.1

A Taxonomy for the Analysis of Trade Sanctions

| Trigger Factor | Total Collapse of Country | | Change of Government | | Significant General Policy Impact | | Significant Specific Policy Impact | | Vengeance | | Strong Diplomatic Protest | | Diplomatic Protest | | Breadth |
|---|---|---|---|---|---|---|---|---|---|---|---|---|---|---|---|
| War | | | | | | | | | | | | | | | U |
| | | | | | | | | | | | | | | | M |
| Threat of War | | | | | | | | | | | | | | | U |
| | | | | | | | | | | | | | | | M |
| Threat to National Security | | | | | | | | | | | | | | | U |
| | | | | | | | | | | | | | | | M |
| Threat to Economic Security | | | | | | | | | | | | | | | U |
| | | | | | | | | | | | | | | | M |
| Historic | | | | | | | | | | | | | | | U |
| | | | | | | | | | | | | | | | M |
| Collective Human Rights | | | | | | | | | | | | | | | U |
| | | | | | | | | | | | | | | | M |
| Individual Human Rights | | | | | | | | | | | | | | | U |
| | | | | | | | | | | | | | | | M |
| Environmental | | | | | | | | | | | | | | | U |
| | | | | | | | | | | | | | | | M |
| | C | D | C | D | C | D | C | D | C | D | C | D | C | D | |

C = Consensus  
D = Discord

Breadth  U = Unilateral  M = Multilateral

Foreign Policy

perhaps to some extent, as working hypotheses for future research.

First, economic sanctions are here to stay. The use of economic sanctions can be expected to increase as economic interdependence increases and the global risks of armed conflict rise. Economic sanctions can be a viable alternative to policies of acquiescence or war and are, under circumstances that appear to offer only a choice between these courses of action, a desirable addition to a national armamentarium.

Second, the imposition of sanctions does not have to be related to the effectiveness of such measures. Imposition is a function of national consensus and of political expediency. Enforcement of sanctions, however, is much more closely related to their effectiveness.

Third, while sanctions are sometimes seen as an inexpensive means for the political leadership to take action, the cost to the domestic communities and the cost of enforcement may be substantial. Although these costs are difficult to determine initially--and, sometimes, even in the long run--they will not become a significant deterrent to sanctions if a national consensus exists on the reasons for and objectives of the sanctions and if some likelihood of achieving the objective exists.

Fourth, under current policy, sanctions are either imposed or not imposed in response to a trigger factor; these alternatives are quite unsophisticated. A gradation--not only of sanction types but also of methods of imposition--could add to a more differentiated use of the threat and impact of this policy measure. Such a differentiation should consist in the gradual build-up of pressure, perhaps through congressional debate or a hearing process, tightly defined in its stages and timing.

Fifth, sanctions need not and cannot be expected to always be multilateral. Divergence among nations should not be allowed to result in a constant return to the lowest common denominator among countries. In order to go beyond the level of symbolic or pseudo-sanctions in a unilateral fashion, however, a national willingness must exist to ensure effectiveness through market activities, for example, the purchase of all supplies of similar products available abroad. The recent purchase of helicopters from Italy may be a portent of things to come.[17]

Sixth, international agreement is easier to obtain on symbolic than on instrumental sanctions, since disagreements on costs are reduced and inequities of trade dependence among nations do not bear heavily on the decision. Considering the relative ease of imposition of such symbolic sanctions and the weaknesses of pseudo-sanctions, it appears that, particularly in the international realm, this type of sanction has so far been insufficiently refined.

Finally, in order to achieve multilateral implementation of instrumental sanctions, objectives need to be clearly defined and sanctions need to be specific. In addition, international consensus can only be achieved if, in international consultations, nations are not talked at or to, but rather are talked with and listened to. Such action also requires the United States to change its stance occasionally. It must be recognized that, given global economic realities, the United States is part of a world economic orchestra in which it can, perhaps, play the role of the first violin, but not any more that of the conductor.

NOTES

1. Margaret P. Doxey, Economic Sanctions and International Enforcement (New York: Oxford University Press, 1980), p. 10.
2. Robin Renwick, Economic Sanctions (Cambridge, MA: Harvard University Press, 1981), p. 11.
3. Doxey, p. 57.
4. Office of Technology Assessment, Technology and East-West Trade: An Update (Washington, DC: U.S. Government Printing Office, 1983), p. 19.
5. Office of Technology Assessment, Technology and East-West Trade (Washington, DC: U.S. Government Printing Office, 1979), p. 112.
6. Richard M. Nixon, Quoted by Lawrence J. Brady in: "Trade Policy," Business Week, November 21, 1983, p. 23.
7. Lawrence J. Brady, "Trade Policy," Business Week, November 21, 1983, p. 23.

8. William A. Root, "Trade Policy," Business Week, November 21, 1983, p. 22.

9. David A. Deese, The Vulnerability of Modern Economies: Economic Diplomacy and World Politics (Philadelphia: Foreign Policy Research Institute, July 13, 1982), p. 9.

10. Office of Technology Assessment, Technology and East-West Trade: An Update, p. 71.

11. Kenneth Abbott, "Linking Trade to Political Goals: Foreign Policy Export Controls in the 1970s and 1980s," Sixty-Five Minnesota Law Review, 1980.

12. Klaus Knorr, Economic Relations as an Instrument of National Power (Philadelphia: Foreign Policy Research Institute, 1982), material taken from original manuscript given to Foreign Policy Association.

13. Knorr.

14. Office of Technology Assessment, Technology and East-West Trade: An Update, p. 20.

15. Wolfgang Hoffmann, "Einfuhrstopp," Die Zeit, September 30, 1983, p. 13.

16. Hans-Dietrich Genscher, "Independence for Namibia is Bonn Priority," The Week in Germany, December 2, 1983, p. 2.

17. Fred Hiatt, "U.S. to Buy Italian-Made Helicopters to Prevent Acquisition by Iranians," The Washington Post, January 21, 1984, p. A9.

# 2

# ECONOMIC SANCTIONS: AN OFTEN USED AND OCCASIONALLY EFFECTIVE TOOL OF FOREIGN POLICY

## Gary Clyde Hufbauer and Jeffrey J. Schott

Since World War II, economic sanctions have gradually become one of the central tools of foreign policy for the United States, the United Kingdom, the Soviet Union, and the Arab League. The growing reliance on economic sanctions is illustrated by Table 2.1.

The table summarizes 99 instances between 1914 and 1983 in which sanctions were used to pursue political goals. Between 1914 and 1945, there were only 12 such uses--mostly in response to border wars and, of course, the two world wars. In the late 1940s and 1950s, there were 20 cases of trade sanctions, many of which were attempts to secure territorial gains. In the 1960s, there were 21 uses of trade controls for various political and economic objectives. Since 1970, sanctions have been imposed 46 times in pursuit of improved respect for human rights, nuclear nonproliferation, expropriation claims, antiterrorism, or in response to military action.

Economic sanctions are seldom imposed in isolation; instead, they are usually one ingredient in a sauce of diplomatic and other measures concocted to induce the target coun-

AUTHORS' NOTE:  This chapter summarizes the findings from the authors' monograph, Economic Sanctions in Support of Foreign Policy Goals, published by the Institute for International Economics in Washington, D.C.

TABLE 2.1

Chronological Summary of Economic Sanctions for Foreign Policy Goals, 1914–83

| Case Number | Principal Sender | Target Country | Active Years | Goals of Sender Country |
|---|---|---|---|---|
| 14–1* | United Kingdom | Germany | 1914–18 | Military victory |
| 17–1* | United States | Japan | 1917 | Use shipping to help Allies in World War I |
| 18–1* | United Kingdom | USSR | 1918–20 | (1) Renew support for Allies in World War I (2) Destabilize Bolshevik regime |
| 21–1* | United Kingdom and League of Nations | Yugoslavia | 1921 | Block Yugoslav attempts to wrest territory from Albania; retain 1913 borders |
| 25–1* | League of Nations | Greece | 1925 | Withdraw from occupation of Bulgarian territory |
| 32–1* | League of Nations | Paraguay, Bolivia | 1932–35 | Settle the Chaco War |
| 33–1* | United Kingdom | USSR | 1933 | Release two British citizens |
| 35–1* | League of Nations | Italy | 1935–36 | Withdraw Italian troops from Ethiopia |
| 38–1* | United Kingdom and United States | Mexico | 1938–47 | Settle expropriation claims |
| 39–1* | Alliance Powers | Germany, later Japan | 1939–45 | Military victory |
| 40–1* | United States | Japan | 1940–41 | Withdraw from Southeast Asia |

(continued)

Table 2.1, continued

| Case Number | Principal Sender | Target Country | Active Years | Goals of Sender Country |
|---|---|---|---|---|
| 44–1* | United States | Argentina | 1944–47 | (1) Remove Nazi influence<br>(2) Destabilize Peron government |
| 46–1* | Arab League | Israel | 1946– | Create a homeland for Palestinians |
| 48–1* | United States | Netherlands | 1948–49 | Recognize Republic of Indonesia |
| 48–2 | India | Hyderabad | 1948 | Assimilate Hyderabad into India |
| 48–3* | USSR | United States, United Kingdom, and France | 1948–49 | (1) Prevent formation of a West German government<br>(2) Assimilate West Berlin into East Germany |
| 48–4* | USSR | Yugoslavia | 1948–55 | (1) Rejoin Soviet camp<br>(2) Destabilize Tito government |
| 48–5* | United States and COCOMa | USSR and COMECONb | 1948– | (1) Deny strategic materials<br>(2) Impair Soviet military potential |
| 49–1 | West Germany | USSR | 1949–69 | Concessions on reunification |
| 49–2* | United States and CHINCOMc | China | 1949–70 | (1) Retaliation for Communist takeover and subsequent assistance to North Korea<br>(2) Deny strategic and other materials |
| 50–1 | United States | North Korea | 1950–53 | Withdraw attack on South Korea |
| 51–1* | United Kingdom and United States | Iran | 1951–53 | (1) Reverse the nationalization of oil facilities<br>(2) Destabilize Mussadiq government |

| Code | Actor | Target | Year | Objective |
|---|---|---|---|---|
| 54-1* | USSR | Australia | 1954 | Repatriate a Soviet defector |
| 54-2 | India | Goa | 1954-61 | Assimilate Goa into India |
| 54-3* | Spain | United Kingdom | 1954– | Gain sovereignty over Gibraltar |
| 56-1* | United States | Israel | 1956 | (1) Withdraw from Sinai; (2) Implement UN Resolution 242; (3) Push Palestinian autonomy talks |
| 56-2 | United Arab Republic | United States and Europe | 1956 | Prompt Israel, UK, and France to withdraw from Sinai and Suez Canal |
| 56-3* | United States | United Kingdom and France | 1956 | Withdraw from Suez |
| 56-4* | United States | Laos | 1956-62 | (1) Destabilize Prince Souvanna Phouma government; (2) Destabilize General Phoumi government; (3) Prevent Communist takeover |
| 57-1* | Indonesia | Netherlands | 1957-62 | Control of West Irian |
| 58-1* | USSR | Finland | 1958-59 | Adopt pro-USSR policies |
| 58-2 | United States | North Vietnam, later Vietnam | 1958– | (1) Impede military effectiveness of North Vietnam; (2) Retribution for aggression in South Vietnam |
| 60-1* | United States | Dominican Republic | 1960-62 | (1) Cease subversion in Venezuela; (2) Destabilize Trujillo government |
| 60-2* | USSR | China | 1960-70 | (1) Retaliation for break with Soviet policy; (2) Destabilize Mao government |

(continued)

Table 2.1, continued

| Case Number | Principal Sender | Target Country | Active Years | Goals of Sender Country |
|---|---|---|---|---|
| 60-3* | United States | Cuba | 1960- | (1) Settle expropriation claims<br>(2) Destabilize Castro government<br>(3) Discourage Cuba from foreign military adventures |
| 61-1* | United States | Ceylon | 1961-65 | Settle expropriation claims |
| 61-2* | USSR | Albania | 1961-82 | (1) Retaliation for alliance with China<br>(2) Destabilize Hoxha government |
| 61-3* | NATO Allies | East Germany | 1961-62 | Berlin Wall |
| 62-1* | United States | Brazil | 1962-64 | (1) Settle expropriation claims<br>(2) Destabilize Goulart government |
| 62-2* | United Nations | South Africa | 1962- | (1) End apartheid<br>(2) Grant independence to Namibia |
| 63-1* | United States | United Arab Republic | 1963-65 | (1) Cease military activity in Yemen and Congo<br>(2) Moderate anti-U.S. rhetoric |
| 63-2* | Indonesia | Malaysia | 1963-67 | Promote "Crush Malaysia" campaign |
| 63-3* | United States | Indonesia | 1963-66 | (1) Cease "Crush Malaysia" campaign<br>(2) Destabilize Sukarno government |
| 63-4 | African states | Portugal | 1963-65 | Leave Africa |
| 65-1* | United States | Chile | 1965-66 | Roll back copper price |

| | | | | |
|---|---|---|---|---|
| 65-2* | United States | India | 1965-67 | Alter policy to favor agriculture |
| 65-3* | United Kingdom and United Nations | Rhodesia | 1965-79 | Majority rule by black Africans |
| 65-4* | United States | Arab League | 1965- | Stop U.S. firms from implementing Arab boycott of Israel |
| 65-5 | USSR | Romania | 1965 | Reduce diplomatic openings to the West |
| 67-1 | Nigeria | Biafra | 1967 | End independence movement |
| 68-1 | United States | Peru | 1968 | Forego aircraft purchases from France |
| 68-2* | United States | Peru | 1968-74 | Settle expropriation claims |
| 68-3 | United States | Brazil | 1968-69 | Restore democracy |
| 70-1* | United States | Chile | 1970-73 | (1) Settle expropriation claims<br>(2) Destabilize Allende government |
| 71-1* | United States | India and Pakistan | 1971 | Cease fighting in East Pakistan (Bangladesh) |
| S-1 | United States | Countries supporting international terrorism | 1972- | Overview |
| 72-2* | United Kingdom and United States | Uganda | 1972-79 | (1) Retaliation for expelling Asians<br>(2) Improve human rights<br>(3) Destabilize Amin government |

(continued)

Table 2.1, continued

| Case Number | Principal Sender | Target Country | Active Years | Goals of Sender Country |
|---|---|---|---|---|
| S-2 | United States | Countries violating human rights | 1973– | Overview |
| 73-1* | Arab League | United States and Netherlands | 1973-74 | (1) Retaliation for supporting Israel in October War<br>(2) Restore pre-1967 Israeli borders |
| 73-2* | United States | South Korea | 1973-77 | Improve human rights |
| 73-3* | United States | Chile | 1973-81 | Improve human rights |
| 74-1* | United States | Turkey | 1974-78 | Withdraw Turkish troops from Cyprus |
| 74-2* | Canada | India | 1974-76 | (1) Deter further nuclear explosions<br>(2) Apply stricter nuclear safeguards |
| 74-3* | Canada | Pakistan | 1974-76 | (1) Apply stricter safeguards to nuclear power plant<br>(2) Forego nuclear reprocessing |
| 75-1* | United States and Canada | South Korea | 1975-76 | Forego nuclear reprocessing |
| 75-2* | United States | USSR | 1975– | Liberalize Jewish emigration |
| 75-3* | United States | Eastern Europe | 1975– | Liberalize Jewish emigration |
| 75-4* | United States | South Africa | 1975– | (1) Adhere to nuclear safeguards<br>(2) Avert explosion of nuclear device |

| | | | | |
|---|---|---|---|---|
| 75-5 | United States | Cambodia | 1975– | (1) Retaliation for North Vietnamese aggression (2) Improve human rights |
| 76-1* | United States | Uruguay | 1976– | Improve human rights |
| 76-2* | United States | Taiwan | 1976-77 | Forego nuclear reprocessing |
| 76-3* | United States | Ethiopia | 1976– | (1) Settle expropriation claims (2) Improve human rights |
| 77-1* | United States | Paraguay | 1977– | Improve human rights |
| 77-2* | United States | Guatemala | 1977-82 | Improve human rights |
| 77-3* | United States | Argentina | 1977-82 | Improve human rights |
| 77-4* | Canada | Japan | 1977-78 | Adhere to nuclear safeguards |
| 77-5* | United States | Nicaragua | 1977-79 | (1) Destabilize Somoza government (2) Improve human rights |
| 77-6 | United States | El Salvador | 1977-81 | Improve human rights |
| 78-1* | China | Albania | 1978-83 | Retaliation for anti-Chinese rhetoric |
| 78-2* | United States | Brazil | 1978-80 | Adhere to nuclear safeguards |
| 78-3* | United States | Argentina | 1978-80 | Adhere to nuclear safeguards |
| 78-4* | United States | India | 1978-80 | Adhere to nuclear safeguards |
| 78-5 | United States | USSR | 1978– | Liberalize treatment of dissidents (e.g., Sharansky) |
| 78-6 | Arab League | Egypt | 1978– | Withdraw from Camp David Process |

(continued)

Table 2.1, continued

| Case Number | Principal Sender | Target Country | Active Years | Goals of Sender Country |
|---|---|---|---|---|
| 78-7 | China | Vietnam | 1978– | Withdraw troops from Cambodia |
| 78-8* | United States | Libya | 1978– | (1) Terminate support of international terrorism<br>(2) Destabilize Qaddafi government |
| 79-1* | United States | Iran | 1979–81 | (1) Release hostages<br>(2) Settle expropriation claims |
| 79-2* | United States | Pakistan | 1979–80 | Adhere to nuclear safeguards |
| 79-3* | Arab League | Canada | 1979–80 | Retaliation for planned move of Canadian Embassy in Israel from Tel Aviv to Jerusalem |
| 80-1* | United States | USSR | 1980– | (1) Withdraw Soviet troops from Afghanistan<br>(2) Impair Soviet military potential |
| 80-2* | United States | Iraq | 1980–82 | Terminate support of international terrorism |
| 81-1* | United States | Nicaragua | 1981– | (1) End support for El Salvador rebels<br>(2) Destabilize Sandinista government |
| 81-2 | USSR | Poland | 1981–82 | Maintain internal discipline |
| 81-3* | United States | Poland | 1981– | (1) Lift martial law<br>(2) Free dissidents<br>(3) Resume talks with Solidarity |

| Case | Imposer | Target | Date | Objective |
|---|---|---|---|---|
| 81-4* | United States | USSR | 1981–82 | (1) Lift martial law in Poland<br>(2) Cancel USSR-Europe pipeline project<br>(3) Impair Soviet economic/military potential |
| 81-6 | European Economic Community | Turkey | 1981–82 | Restore democracy |
| 82-1* | United Kingdom | Argentina | 1982 | Withdraw troops from Falkland Islands |
| 82-2 | Arab League | Zaire | 1982 | Withdraw recognition of Israel |
| 82-3* | Netherlands | Surinam | 1982– | (1) Improve human rights<br>(2) Limit alliance with Cuba<br>(3) Destabilize Bouterse government |
| 82-4 | South Africa | Lesotho | 1982– | Return refugees suspected of antistate activities |
| 83-1 | Australia | France | 1983– | Stop nuclear testing in the South Pacific |

*Asterisks denote cases abstracted to date included in the economic and political analysis in this monograph. The abstracts of these and the remaining cases will be published in Gary Clyde Hufbauer, Jeffrey J. Schott, and Kimberly Ann Elliott, Economic Sanctions Reconsidered: History and Current Policy (Washington, D.C.: Institute for International Economics, forthcoming).

aCOCOM = Coordinating Committee for Multilateral Export Controls.

bCOMECON = Council for Mutual Economic Assistance.

try to change its policies or practices. Recent years have seen a dramatic upswing both in the total number of cases where sanctions have been imposed and in the number of cases where military action was not part of the sauce.

The major economic powers make greatest use of the weapon. In 51 of the 99 cases documented in the summary table, the United States has been the principal country imposing the sanction, often with the grudging cooperation of its allies. Over half of the U.S. actions have been taken since 1970. Other significant users of trade sanctions have been the United Kingdom (seven instances prewar, eight postwar); the Soviet Union (nine uses, often against recalcitrant satellites); and the Arab League (four uses of its newfound oil muscle).

Since 1950, the goals of U.S. foreign policy have shifted to reflect changing international concerns. Sanction tools have been reshaped as well. U.S. bilateral aid no longer looms as large in world financial flows as it once did, and U.S. officials find it increasingly difficult to maneuver policy decisions in the World Bank and the International Monetary Fund to suit American political interests. Consequently, the denial of bilateral and multilateral aid, which served as an effective tool in the 1960s, has given way in the 1970s and 1980s to the denial of trade and commercial finance.

Despite change in targets and tools, U.S. sanctions have been deployed throughout the postwar period to serve three broad purposes: to demonstrate resolve at home and abroad, to punish target countries (supposedly deterring them and others from future outrages and misdeeds), and to alter the offensive policies of foreign governments. Faced with political demands for action, U.S. presidents have often found that the alternatives to economic sanctions—military action or diplomatic protest—are either too strong or too weak.

Whatever satisfaction the imposition of sanctions may bring at home, it often fails to alter the offensive policies of governments abroad. Great fanfare surrounding the imposition of economic sanctions can create a backlash effect. The publicity may galvanize the target country into political cohesion, and a failure to achieve demonstrable policy changes can irritate both allies abroad and constituents at home who bear the economic burden of the sanctions. These backlash problems can become particularly serious when there is little hope of coercing a change of policy from the target country—

as in the League of Nations' ill-fated use of sanctions against Italy in 1935-36 or the more recent U.S. actions against the Soviet Union and Poland.

Sanctions are rarely, if ever, effective in achieving "high" policy goals against major foreign powers. For example, sanctions are rarely successful in impairing the military potential of a strong target country or causing such a country to alter its fundamental internal policies (such as emigration control or apartheid). Research findings indicate that 19 "high policy" episodes have been launched since 1914, and sanctions made an important contribution to a successful outcome only in the two world wars.

To justify even a remote hope for success in "high" policy cases, sender countries must form a near monopoly over trade relations with the target country. This obvious precept, learned in World War I and World War II, was forgotten in the case of the United Nations sanctions against Rhodesia and South Africa, and it was turned on its head in the recent U.S. sanctions to block construction of the Soviet-European gas pipeline.

If, however, the target country is internally weak or has no supporting alliances with major world powers, sanctions can force limited policy changes and can even destabilize governments. When sanctions have contributed to the outcome desired by the sender country, usually the objective has been narrowly defined--as in the case of the asset freezes instituted by the United States against Iran and by the United Kingdom against Argentina--or the target government has already been weakened by other events, as happened prior to the destabilization of governments in Finland, the Dominican Republic, and Chile. Of the 64 cases studied in these categories, sanctions achieved a degree of success in 30 episodes.

Economic coercion works best if applied with surgical authority and speed. A heavy, slow hand invites both evasion and the mobilization of domestic opinion in the target country: the sanctions are likely to be undercut either by the sender country's own firms or by foreign competitors; more important, they may serve to strengthen the target government as it appeals to the forces of nationalism. The experience with recent U.S. sanctions against Nicaragua demonstrates this point. Sanctions applied in a measured and deliberate manner only unified Nicaragua in support of the

Sandinista government.  Domestic opposition to the Sandinistas was suppressed, and Nicaragua became more resourceful in finding ways around escalating U.S. pressure.

The success of the Iranian asset freeze and the aid-denial cases of the 1960s involving Egypt, Brazil, India, and other countries suggest that financial sanctions are generally more effective than trade sanctions.  Private financiers who might provide an alternative source of credit must rely on a long-term relationship with the target country, and long-term relations are unsettled when financial sanctions are in the air.  Moreover, the denial of finance can disrupt the well-laid plans of powerful government ministers.

As the examples cited illustrate, much can be learned from historical experience with economic sanctions.  Some of that learning is summarized in the form of "nine commandments."

First, don't bite off more than you can chew.  Sanctions can work if used judiciously to reach modest, carefully defined objectives.  Sanctions cannot move mountains or coerce adversaries into making major changes in their domestic policies (e.g., apartheid in South Africa).

Second, do not pick on someone your own size.  In successful cases, the target country is usually much smaller in economic terms than the country imposing the sanctions. Sanctions generally do not help in big power confrontations.

Third, do pick on the weak and helpless.  Weak countries, with unstable regimes and shaky economies, are more susceptible to economic coercion.  Successful cases build on weakness, not strength.

Fourth, do impose the maximum cost on your adversary. Sanctions that bite are sanctions that work.  This study found that the costs inflicted by sanctions were equal to almost 2 percent of the gross national product of target countries in successful cases, as compared to only 0.6 percent in failures.

Fifth, do apply sanctions decisively and with resolution.  The longer sanctions are in force, the less likely they will succeed.  A policy of "gradually tightening the screws" gives the target country time to find alternate suppliers, to build new alliances, and to rally domestic support behind government policies.

Sixth, do not pay too high a price for sanctions. Actions that impose major costs on domestic industries erode support for sanctions. A country does not hurt its adversary by shooting itself in the foot.

Seventh, do not suppose that, where sanctions will fail, companion policies will necessarily succeed. There is no evidence that economic sanctions used in combination with covert and quasi-military measures had a particularly high success rate.

Eighth, do not exaggerate the role of international cooperation. Support from one's allies always helps, but a country does not need extensive support when it pursues modest and specific goals. Where cooperation is essential--as in "high policy" East-West cases--the goals are usually more ambitious and therefore less likely to be reached. International cooperation is unlikely to tip the scales toward success in these difficult cases, though it can limit the costs.

Finally, do plan carefully. A little planning can go a long way toward crafting an effective sanctions policy. Planning can increase the chance of achieving foreign policy goals, save embarrassment with domestic constituencies and foreign allies, and make the task of dismantling sanctions easier when, as usually happens, tempers cool and foreign policy objectives have not been achieved.

In 1983, a good deal of congressional attention was devoted to the renewal of the Export Administration Act (EAA) and its relation to economic sanctions. Three specific questions raised in the EAA debate focus attention on ways sanctions can be implemented more effectively:

1. Should the President be required to demonstrate that substitute goods are not available from third countries when he restricts exports on national security or foreign policy grounds? This is the foreign availability question.
2. Should the EAA be amended to allow the President the power to limit imports as an economic sanction?
3. Should preexisting contracts be honored when sanctions are imposed? This is the sanctity of contract question.

With regard to the question of foreign availability, national security export controls can hardly achieve their narrow goal of restricting foreign access to military hardware when the same goods are available from third countries.

One can only applaud procedures that would give U.S. exporters an effective opportunity to protest export restrictions
if the same goods are being shipped from France or Japan.

When controls are imposed for foreign policy reasons,
one comes to different conclusions. The success of foreign
policy controls does not depend on completely cutting off the
adversary's trade or means of finance. Rather, success depends on seeking well-defined and suitably modest goals and
inflicting significant costs on the target country. Foreign
availability is not the issue--the issue is whether the sanctions imposed are equal to the goals sought.

As to the question of import controls, some congress-
men would like to expand presidential authority to limit imports from foreign countries--allies and adversaries alike.
Restricting U.S. imports from allies as a means of enforcing
national security controls would amount to waging economic
war on many fronts, rendering ultimate success all the more
elusive. Limiting imports from adversaries, however, would
probably achieve foreign policy goals at least as often as
export controls.

There is a risk, however, that the creation of a new
tool would invite its use. Moreover, import controls could
spawn vested domestic groups urging their continuance. Imagine, for example, a Steel and Textile Coalition for Human
Rights in Korea.

With regard to the question of contract sanctity, sanctions are most likely to be effective when they are imposed
with maximum force. Incremental sanctions, by contrast,
create their antidotes. The more existing contracts are
honored, the less scope for sudden imposition of maximum
measures--thereby undercutting the initial impact of sanctions and lessening the ultimate chance for success.

On the other hand, the cancellation of existing contracts makes the affected U.S. firms certain opponents of
the entire policy. Why should they pay a special "tax" for
the conduct of foreign policy? In an open society, domestic
disaffection can quickly corrode foreign policy.

To resolve this dilemma, Congress might require the
U.S. government, in carefully defined situations, to compensate U.S. industrial workers and firms for wages and profits
lost when sanctions are imposed. Farmers are now protected
against future sanctions. Should industry receive less?

The EAA debate was important.  It focused attention on
the proper use of economic power to conduct foreign policy.
But in the end, as the "nine commandments" suggest, the effective use of sanctions will depend less on fine-tuned
legislation than on the wisdom and restraint of the President in deploying this tool of foreign policy.

# 3

# THE STRATEGIC DIMENSIONS OF TRADE: A FRAMEWORK FOR DISCUSSION

## Richard F. Kaufman

The use of trade controls strikes a lot of people as the wrong way for an economic system based on free-enterprise market principles to behave, but there are national security considerations and there are other factors that have contributed to a system of controls. Controls are a fact of life, but so is East-West trade. This chapter tries to set the stage for the book as a whole by touching on some very broad questions and issues to develop a framework based on the strategic dimensions of trade.

Initially, one needs to say something about the word "strategic," which is used in different ways for different purposes. In the dialogue over East-West trade policy, one hears references to strategic requirements and to strategic items of trade and, sometimes in the same breath, references to militarily relevant trade. Such phrases often reflect a blurring of the distinction between what is of strategic importance and what is of military importance. The two are related but not identical. Further, exports of advanced technology are not inherently more strategic than any other exports simply because they embody sophisticated materials or processes or because they have dual-use characteristics.

What is of strategic importance depends on how one defines strategic. There are two common usages for this word. The first is a narrow one that relates to the art of projecting and directing the large military movements and

34

operations of a campaign, as opposed to the tactics that go
into the numerous battles of a campaign or of a war. A
broader definition is the utilization, during peace and
during war, of all of a nation's resources through large-
scale, long-range planning and development to ensure security. Both uses of strategic are linked to the idea of
security, although in vastly different ways and with varying
effects on policy.

The issue at hand is whether trade with the Soviet
Union enhances or diminishes U.S. security. This issue can
be restated in two ways by asking two contrasting types of
questions. One is whether it is possible to preserve security while trading with the Soviet Union. The second way
is whether it is possible to conduct trade with the Soviet
Union in a way that enhances U.S. security.

Those who use the first formulation would probably
prefer a narrower definition of strategic, or would emphasize the narrow definition of strategic, and would argue
that any trade that strengthens the Soviet economy also
strengthens its military capacity and therefore increases
the threat to U.S. security. This argument makes assump-
tions about the relationships between trade, economic growth,
and military capabilities that seem plausible but are difficult if not impossible to prove. Those who would use the
second formulation would prefer the broader definition of
strategic and would argue that, in light of international
economic interdependencies and the political requirements
of NATO, trade with the Soviet Union and other communist
states can and does enhance U.S. security interests. This
argument, too, is difficult to prove.

Conceivably, it might be possible to enhance our security by denying the Soviets access to Western markets, assuming that would retard Soviet economic growth and military
capabilities. In view of the existence of the U.S.-Soviet
long-term grain agreement and the other East-West trade relationships of ourselves and our allies, the practical question is how to develop an East-West trade policy that bears
a logical relationship to U.S. strategy toward the Soviet
Union. As the United States has followed several trade policies and strategic approaches since World War II, a look
backward may shed some light on the problem. This history
can be divided into three periods.

The first was a period of trade denial during the Cold War. During this period, the United States and all other Western industrial countries followed policies that held trade with the Soviet Union to a bare minimum. The policy of denial was followed from the end of World War II until the early 1960s.

The second period began with the easing of U.S.-Soviet relations under Presidents Kennedy and Johnson and ended with the policy of detente adopted by President Nixon. During this period, steps were taken toward normalization of trade relations. Elsewhere in the West, a similar policy was adopted, somewhat independently of the United States, as exemplified by West Germany's Ostpolitik.

In recent years, East-West economic relations have become more complicated and there has been a divergence of U.S. and West European policies. As U.S.-Soviet political and military frictions intensified in the last part of the 1970s, President Jimmy Carter responded to Soviet provocation, such as human rights violations, with selective restrictions on the trade of computer equipment and gas equipment. Following the Soviet invasion of Afghanistan, Carter imposed an embargo on the sale of grain to the Soviet Union. Although President Reagan lifted the grain embargo, he continued the policy of limited sanctions, imposing them against the Soviet gas pipeline following Poland's declaration of martial law. In the meantime, Washington's allies supported the Carter sanctions lukewarmly at best, and there was open dissension over the Reagan sanctions, especially the attempt to apply extraterritoriality.

At present, there are two approaches toward relations with the Soviets and East-West trade. To oversimplify just a little, the West Europeans still believe in a modified form of detente, while the United States has edged closer to Cold War. It remains to be seen whether the United States continues to employ selective sanctions while its allies continue trading or whether we work at a more unified approach. In the meantime, it seems apparent that the United States is taking a narrower approach to strategy than is Western Europe.

A few observations should be made based on this brief framework. In the first place, there is no question about the need for national security controls on military equipment and militarily relevant trade. On the other hand, the United States no longer is the economically and technologically dominant nation. It can no longer call the tune for its allies on trade policy, and our allies do not always agree with our definition of what is militarily relevant or strategic" trade.

Second, Western industrialized countries are unwilling to return to a policy of economic isolation, and the Eastern countries, led by the Soviet Union, are equally unwilling to isolate themselves from the West. Western Europeans believe that East-West trade has been mutually beneficial and that detente has been successful as both a militarily and politically stabilizing factor. The Carter and Reagan sanctions were economically ineffective and politically divisive, both in the United States and NATO. Our allies are not likely to join us in any future use of sanctions affecting significant aspects of their own trade, except perhaps on a very temporary basis.

With respect to economic leverage over the Soviet Union, policymakers need to recognize that the Soviet economy is not in a crisis; it is not about to collapse. In fact, it is experiencing somewhat of a recovery, or a resurgence, at the present time, although it is unclear how long it will continue. The USSR's annual rate of gross national product growth, which has been quite low--averaging 1 or 2 percent over the past four years--will be in the range of 3.5 to 4 percent in 1983 and is projected to average between 2 and 3 percent over the next several years. Trade between the Soviet Union and the West is expected to continue growing for the remainder of the decade. In view of the small share of this trade attributable to the United States, and the fact that most advanced technology is available from sources other than the United States, our ability to affect or impede Soviet economic trends is minimal at best.

Soviet economic problems are mostly due to factors beyond the Soviet government's control, such as weather conditions, demographic trends, and the high cost of extracting and transporting natural resources from remote areas. Foreign trade with the Soviet Union cannot cure these problems for the Soviets, nor can it reduce the numerous inefficiencies--including the inefficient transfer of technology--

caused by the highly bureaucratized, overregulated centrally
planned system. So long as the United States is unable to
impede substantially the Soviet economy, unilateral restrictions, while they may have some moral or symbolic value
to Americans, have the practical effect of harming mostly
the United States private sector, with the result that
Eastern markets are handed over to other Western industrial
countries.

Market forces are a factor of growing importance in
the making of foreign economic policy. The U.S. agricultural trade with the Soviet Union, a trade that the political leadership would probably prefer not to support, is a
case of producer preferences influencing political decision
making about trade policy. This factor is evident in West
European energy purchases from the Soviet Union and in the
exports of technology and equipment to the Soviet Union
throughout the industrialized West. The effects of market
forces are making it difficult for U.S. firms in the trade
community to remain aloof from East-West policy regardless
of whether they are directly engaged in trade with the
East. American business executives are coming to realize
that East-West trade cannot be walled off from other foreign trade. Private-sector pressures on Washington to get
the government's foreign trade policy house in order, to
place East-West trade on a more rational and explicit
basis, and to make our policies more consistent with those
of our allies will probably increase.

The divergence of East-West trade policies between
the United States and its allies is a product in part of
disagreements over the relationship between trade with the
Soviet Union, Soviet economic growth, and Soviet military
capabilities; in part of disagreements over the ability
of the West to influence Soviet economic growth; and in
part of disagreements over whether it is in the interest of
the West to normalize trade relations with the East. In
the United States, policy has been on an unsteady course,
debated acrimoniously, and changed frequently. The resigna-
tion in the fall of 1983 of two senior East-West officials
in the Commerce and State departments, the frequent reor-
ganizations of East-West trade responsibilities within
the executive branch, and the disagreements over policy

among the State, Defense, and Commerce departments suggest
the lack of an orderly process for making East-West trade
policy and of a cohesive, well-thought-out policy that fits
into an overall strategy toward the Soviet Union.

# 4

# OBJECTIVES AND GOALS OF U.S. EXPORT CONTROL POLICY

## Lionel Olmer

As of last evening, information available to me indicated that both Senators from Alaska have put a hold on Senate consideration of the Export Administration Act, wanting to have hearings on the question of the removal from the act of the short supply prohibition on the export of Alaskan crude oil. Pending satisfaction of their request for hearings, the bill is going nowhere on the Senate side; the House may take action sometime next week, but even that's not likely to produce a completed, agreed-upon piece of legislation before the present law expires.

I guess I'd like to preface what I was going to say with a comment on the introductory remarks by the program coordinator, and that is there can be no controls without a cost, and place out of your mind, now and forever, any other possibility. If we are going to have an export control program--and I believe it is essential that this government have one--we have to be prepared to explain the costs to those in our society who have to pay those costs. Maybe we haven't done as good a job as we should or could in this respect; maybe no one ever has. Maybe it is impossible to satisfy the legitimate concerns of the American business community--including the workers, the managers, the shareholders--as to why they've got to suffer a loss, but loss they will suffer if the program is going to be effective, and that's just that.

Now, as to what I had prepared to say. Try to keep in mind during the course of today's seminar that there are several kinds of export controls, and don't mix and match them. There's a national security control section in the Export Administration Act, there is a foreign policy section, there's a short supply section, and I haven't, in either of those three, mentioned one that is as onerous as any other provision in any part of the act to the American business community, about which no debate has taken place during the entire course of the last year, and that's the antiboycott section.

Each of the three sections I mention--national security, foreign policy, and short supply--has to be examined with respect to the objectives it seeks to achieve. You may or may not say it's worth having them, irrespective of whether they achieve those objectives, as in the case of our antiboycott program. No one has made the case that we are going to change Arab behavior toward Israel, and yet we are not advancing the notion that because of that fact we should eliminate the antiboycott program. I'm not proposing it, I don't contemplate it, I don't think it would be proper to do so. In other words, some parts of a control program are there for the purpose of either making the society feel good, as in an expression of criticism against a foreign policy one doesn't like, that one feels is injurious to the conduct of foreign affairs of one's own government or that of one's allies, or one that you simply wish to distance yourself and your people from, as in the case of apartheid in South Africa.

In any event, there are different standards by which one could even hope to judge the effectiveness or the value of an export control program. At the same time, bear in mind a distinction between management of the system--that is, you may not like the way we run the system--and the need for the system itself.

With respect to the national security component of the Export Administration Act, the principal objective is to prevent or to delay--and to delay I mean significantly delay--the possession by adversaries or prospective adversaries of a military capability--a military-industrial capability--they wouldn't otherwise have been able to acquire. It is not to prevent indefinitely; we would be satisfied, in most instances, if a significant delay was achieved by controls.

Another point I'd like to make is that it is growingly evident that to be effective, controls have to be multilateral in character, especially with respect to the national security component of the bill. Clearly it would be desirable if everyone joined forces, whether it be for foreign policy or for national security controls, but I would make the case that in the foreign policy area--when you are in the business of sending signals, when you are in the business of distancing yourself from hateful regimes, when you are trying to make an expression of criticism--surely it is highly desirable to have the expression be multilateral in character. But if it can't be, we hold ourselves to the highest ethical standard and not to the lowest common denominator. So we must be prepared to go it alone in those few instances where, in our President's judgment, our leadership responsibilities to the Western world so require.

With respect to national security controls, it is increasingly evident that, to be effective, it is essential that the controls be multilateral in character. There are very few technologies and products that are uniquely possessed by the United States, so unilateral controls cannot prevent the acquisition of technology by adversaries. Now, having said that, there may be times when, for a short period, it is desirable to unilaterally control, even when you don't have the unique capability, as in the case of letting your allies know the seriousness of your purpose in achieving common agreement. I would argue that these instances should be for a limited period; but the counter to that is we only hurt the U.S. business executive and that foreign competitors are delighted with unilateral restraints.

Just two more points. One is that while there has been this growing evidence of the relative ineffectiveness of unilateral controls, there has been a concomitant growing awareness of the importance of exports to the American economy and to the health of American society. More and more jobs are dependent on our having a competitive industrial base. More and more it is a requisite of preeminence in technology that we have access to foreign markets and that this access be assured for American industry. And to achieve that result, we have to make certain that the United States is seen as a reliable supplier, that the United States has open markets, and that U.S. goods and technology are the best that money can buy.  To do this, we have to have a consistent, predictable policy that represents at its base a consensus.  In the last two and a half years, I've only met one business executive who has tried to argue that it is not practical to control technology because technology is so dynamic that by the time you print the control, somebody is already making inroads on it; that it's available elsewhere, and all you're doing is penalizing the long-suffering U.S. business executive.  Everyone else in the business community-- and you'll have to accept on faith that I have spent a fair amount of time reaching out (to the extent they haven't reached out to find me) for conversations with American business executives--acknowledges the need for national security controls.  And most of them will accept it patriotically, genuinely, and with utter sincerity.

The vast bulk of U.S. business executives recognize the importance to the United States of maintaining the national security export control program.  We spend an incredible amount of money on weapons systems.  And we know, without a shadow of a doubt, that the Soviets have made, are making, and will continue to make an aggressive effort to acquire Western technology.  The evidence is just overwhelming that they do and that they've been successful in that process.  It makes little sense for us to continue spending this vast treasure on defense and to permit, simultaneously, the transfer of technology that will enable the Soviets to defeat our weapons systems, maybe even sometimes without our foreknowledge, so that we can't even develop a countermeasure.  And that has happened.

Export controls are a necessary part of life in the era in which we find ourselves, and I'd like to close with a comment about the nature of the technological revolution that has occurred.  Ten to 15 years ago, the leading edge of technology was represented by defense weapons systems.  Their procurement led American industry into new fields of endeavor in research and in development and ultimately into production.

That has been less true over the course of the last decade.  The private sector today is the driving element in the development of new technology.  You need only look at the microelectronics revolution to observe that, even in private homes today, there is more computing power than was

available in the United States a little more than a generation ago. What that means is that the problem of control
has become more complicated by an order of magnitude because
the Defense Department is not the sole possessor of, nor
does it have the leverage it once had over, the productive
capacity of U.S. industry that is turning out high technology.

Now some would say that the problem is therefore so
complicated, so sophisticated, and so pervasive that we
should just forget about it. And I would say to you, we
can't afford to forget. We can't afford to because the
stakes are so large. The effort we are making is relatively
costless. The pain to the American industry of the controls
that have been in effect has not been that onerous. If anything, our relationship in the Western alliance in the area
of national security controls is improved, not impaired, because of our mutual efforts. The allies are in total agreement with us within COCOM--and several other like-minded
nations that are not members of COCOM--that technology and
products that have a military potential should not be exported to adversaries or prospective adversaries. Our differences are over the technical characteristics and over the
management of the system, but not as regards the fact that
it is essential to us.

So, if I sound somewhat contradictory, I meant to be.
I meant to point out the difficulty, the increasing difficulty, that governments have in developing understandable,
predictable, and reliable controls. But that doesn't mean
we shouldn't try. We have to try. It becomes increasingly
important that we do a better job at it.

# 5

# DEVELOPING MULTILATERAL TRADE CONTROLS

## William E. Brock

From time to time, we are very forcibly reminded that, in the real world, one has to deal with people for whom one has less than full respect—people who are, at a minimum, adversaries, whose representatives have openly and publicly declared that the only morality they recognize is one that will further world communism. Few of us needed the example of the Korean Air Lines atrocity to understand the kind of people with which this country has to deal.

The question of what kind of commercial relationships one can establish with an adversarial society that has a totally different and inadequate set of ethical, moral, so- cial, and economic values is not simple, and there probably are no simple answers. One thing is clear, however; what- ever this country does, it should try to do it multilater- ally. That is a benchmark of any logical approach.

The United States and its allies have agreed to study the full range of East-West economic relations in a search for the most reasonable approach to the issue. The Organi- zation of Economic Cooperation and Development (OECD) is now examining the special problems that arise in dealing with the state trading companies of the East. NATO is preparing analyses of the security implications of East-West economic relations. COCOM is analyzing the question of whether mem- bers' security interest require controls on additional high technology items, and the OECD and the International Energy

Agency (IEA) are giving special attention to energy dependence in their county-by-country reviews.

United States policy, which is derived from these
exercises, is fairly straightforward. Washington differentiates between friends and adversaries. It has done so
and shall continue to do so, at least while the Reagan
administration is in office. For example, China, although
possessing an economic system different from ours, not only
has received most-favored-nation treatment from the United
States, as other friendly countries do, but also is on the
verge of an entirely new relationship in the high technology
area, both with the United States and with some of its principal allies. Even a member of the Warsaw Pact, such as
Hungary, can receive most-favored-nation treatment based on
its recent human rights record. Another Warsaw Pact member, Romania, not only receives most-favored-nation status
but also gets a tariff preference as a less developed country for importation of its products.

The contrast between U.S. trade relations with China,
Hungary, and Romania and, alternatively, with Poland and
the Soviet Union has become increasingly stark. For several
years, Poland has failed to live up to its General Agreement
on Tariffs and Trade (GATT) obligations. The U.S. policy
was one of restraint and understanding, hoping that internal
developments would lead to improved human rights for Polish
citizens and a resumption of Polish obligations under the
GATT. After the banning of Solidarity, President Reagan
concluded that the policy of restraint was no longer reasonable. He decided that the United States should no longer
look the other way, but should witness the fact that respect
for human rights in Poland was declining. When Poland refused to meet its previously agreed to GATT contract, the
United States withdrew most-favored-nation status. Poland
clearly was not in compliance with its trade and other
obligations.

The Soviet Union has not received most-favored-nation
status for over 30 years. President Reagan has banned
Aeroflot from this country and has closed the Soviets' New
York trade office. The United States, it is clear, deals
with the Soviet Union solely on an arm's-length basis. It
has concluded that a prudent approach to U.S.-Soviet trade
is most appropriate, and it has refrained from granting

preferential treatment to the Soviets, preferring instead to rely on market forces.

This series of historical facts is designed to illustrate two things. First, the United States has consciously sought, particularly in the last year, to arrive at a common understanding--a common policy--with the principal free nations of the world on how to deal with East-West trade; we think that is a more effective and logical policy. Second, the United States is willing to differentiate between Eastern countries that have different stands of morality and different policies on accepting contractual, ethical, and legal obligations. The Reagan administration hopes that both friends and adversaries understand that the United States would welcome any improvement in the situation, but there are limits to how far it will go. The United States simply will not violate its principles when there is no responsible action on the part of an adversary nation.

The Reagan administration has worked hard to approach East-West trade multilaterally, in a spirit of cooperation with our allies. The clear and overwhelming preference is for unified action. There are times, however, when this country will take unilateral action because it feels it has no alternative. Such actions should be taken only as a last resort. An example that is fairly fresh in most of our minds and that goes back to a difficult and painful debate is the pipeline sanctions of a year ago. In retrospect, it is clear that all of us could have done better had we been communicating for ten years before that event. Instead, the United States and its allies had been drawing a few inches apart each year in their views of East-West trade relations, and the frustration was growing on both sides of the Atlantic. Washington and its friends in Europe had not been communicating very well at all for several years before the pipeline controversy. If it had not been the pipeline, something else would have brought us to the consequences of those events.

The pipeline controversy was painful, but the positive aspect of it was that we started talking again, not talking at each other, but with each other, and communicating as people will do when they have a problem. That may be a very important positive change.

Some have argued that the United States tried to make the European allies toe the line on the economic sanctions over the pipeline. Clearly, though, Washington was not trying to do this. It was simply saying, "let's agree on what we agreed on. Let's quit going through the charade of meeting and talking past each other without communicating."

Maybe part of it, or a large part of it, was the fault of the United States. But the degree of frustration in this country prior to the summer of 1982 was fairly intense because of the actions on the part of some Europeans in subsidizing the Soviet Union. This country does not understand that subsidization: we have not understood it for a long time. Not all European governments subsidize the Soviets, but enough did to get the attention of the United States. And the United States was unable to get anybody to sit down and talk about the issue. It could not get anybody to look at COCOM, no progress was being made there.

Many American officials are tired of going to international meetings and having friends stand up and say to Europeans: "I'm from Brazil, or I'm from Turkey, and I don't understand why you are selling sophisticated equipment to the Soviet Union at below-market prices and providing credit for over seven, eight or ten years at half the interest rate you are charging me. You are charging me a higher price for the equipment and you are charging me a higher interest rate, and then you criticize me for not making payments on my loans." It is hard to explain to the Brazils of the world why that was going on. And it is hard to explain to a lot of people in this country why that was going on. But it was true. And as long as it was true and we could not communicate about it, something was going to blow. And it did.

Many Europeans have argued that they did not understand what the United States was saying during the pipeline controversy. We were saying that we would prefer to take actions multilaterally but will do things unilaterally if necessary. Ever since then, U.S. officials have said that, now that discussions have begun on the problem, the United States and Europe should work together. It is not easy; friendship and partnership require contributions from both sides. The United States is capable of making that contribution; it has proved that for the past 200 years and will prove for the next 200 years.

Unfortunately, if a situation similar to the one that brought about the pipeline controversy develops again, similar conflict and tension are going to arise because of the absence of any real exchange of emotional, physical, and intellectual thoughts. The United States is saying: "If you want to subsidize somebody in order to do business, why not subsidize the poor people of the world? Why do you have to subsidize the Soviet Union when it is threatening you militarily?"

The other point that needs to be stressed is one that was mentioned earlier. The United States--and the Europeans--can gain economically without sacrificing security interests by consciously trying to eliminate or reduce trade barriers between the West and those countries that are willing to live by a higher moral standard. This does not exclude countries that happen to have a different economic system. One of the great things that has happened in the last few years is that people have had a chance to see the failure of socialism first hand. They have learned something. They may still call themselves socialists, but every one of them is climbing over every wall in order to move toward more of a market system. We should find a way to give those countries that are willing to exercise that kind of integrity a greater prospect for success. That, by example, will show others that it can be done.

In conclusion, it is doubtful that we ever can or ever will separate economic and political questions. Concepts such as linkage are necessary because one can never separate the actions of people in one area from their actions in other areas. That concept is important in the sense of devising a responsive policy. With the understanding that we are dealing with people with fundamentally different values, we still all live in the world some people call a global village. We must avoid igniting the surface.

# II

# PERSPECTIVES ON TRADE
# WITH ADVERSARIES

Part II moves away from the discussion of the objectives and goals of trade controls and examines the various perspectives of some of the actors most involved in controls. Chapters in the section explain how business executives, politicians, academics, and others view trade controls and the entire issue of East-West trade. Part II illustrates some of the fundamental philosophical differences among actors that makes the issue of export controls such a difficult one to resolve.

Kempton B. Jenkins examines the business perspective of trade with adversaries. He begins by examining some of the major factors affecting international trade today and discusses how those factors affect the corporate view of East-West trade. Jenkins then moves on to note that the failure of trade controls--as demonstrated in the recent U.S. grain embargo and gas pipeline sanctions--has prompted business executives to work together to ease restrictions on trade. He argues that such restrictions, while necessary at times, can be loosened without much worry because American business executives know how to deal with the Soviet Union.

Neil C. Livingstone looks at the politics of East-West trade, arguing that it is naive to think that political and economic considerations can be divorced. At the same time, he argues, it is just as naive to assume that trade controls will be effective. Rather than use trade controls to punish improper Soviet behavior, Livingstone calls for the development of a two-tiered system involving trade with the Soviets and firmness in the face of aggression. He then calls for a public relations campaign to promote trade interests in this country.

Miles M. Costick's chapter takes a far different stance, arguing that trade cannot be conducted freely with the Soviet Union. He argues that the Soviets view trade as a strategic weapon with which to make the West dependent, and he asserts that the West must view trade as a strategic asset to be used as a weapon against the Soviet threat. In his view,

trade is an instrument of the government, and trade controls
are an essential part of the East-West struggle.

The final chapter in the section is by John F. Dealy.
Dealy devotes most of his attention to examining U.S. export
control policy in light of the policies of other countries.
For example, he argues that controls on high technology exports hurt U.S. businesses but do not prevent Soviet acquisition of the technology because of foreign availability. Dealy
argues that U.S. policymakers need to take foreign country
policies more into consideration when determining U.S. trade
control policy.

# 6

# THE BUSINESS PERSPECTIVE OF TRADE WITH ADVERSARIES

## Kempton B. Jenkins

A number of basic realities that have emerged since World War II provide the framework within which corporations must look at trade opportunities with adversary nations. As World War II ended, the United States and the Soviet Union were left as the strongest countries in the world, and polarization between Washington and Moscow increased. That polarization remains today and has a basic effect on trade patterns around the world. In recent years, however, the emergence of new, bizarre adversaries like Qaddafi's Libya, and the increase in adversary by proxy (Marxist Nicaragua, for example) has made that simple polarization more difficult to identify. In discussing trade with adversaries today, one must distinguish between the Soviet Union, on the one hand, and China, Yugoslavia, Romania, Nicaragua, Libya, Syria, and Vietnam, on the other hand. Even some of our political and military allies, such as Japan, are among our most contentious economic adversaries. It is difficult if not impossible, therefore, to arrive at an agreed definition on who the adversaries are. Those concerned with trade policy need to recognize the complexity of determining the various adversarial roles in which the United States finds itself with different countries.

Nonetheless, there is broad agreement that the U.S.-Soviet relationship, which dominates Washington's national security concerns, is an adversarial one. Everyone has a common understanding of the parameters of that relationship; beyond that, it becomes more complicated.

While Moscow and Washington have remained adversaries since World War II, the dominant factor controlling the realities of trade, even more than the United States' relationship with the Soviet Union, has been the globalization of the marketplace. Where once the U.S. domestic market was virtually the only market of interest to U.S. industry, today fungibility is reality. With the incredible boom in high technology and the increasing velocity in lateral transfer and exchange of technology, virtually every major country now has the capacity, through investment, to produce almost any international commodity. This change has eroded any hope for simple unilateral U.S. control of international trade and has created the need for much greater emphasis on alliance politics and the development of consensus among the nations of the free world.

Another basic reality affecting trade has been the deterioration of the U.S. dominance of industrial production. In 1945, the United States stood alone in the world with a highly developed industrial machine prepared to produce seemingly endless quantities of the world's needs. The United States, in fact, faced a serious crisis throughout the 1950s because of its overwhelming balance-of-payments advantage. Beginning in the 1960s, however, the rest of the world began to catch up, as the United States' unprecedented economic largess stimulated first Europe and then Japan. In the last decade, the countries at the rim of the Pacific--South Korea, Taiwan, Hong Kong, and Singapore--entered the competition, and today Brazil, Spain, India, Trinidad and Tobago, and others are joining the industrialized community. Yesterday's balance-of-payments surplus has become an unprecedented, almost disastrous 1983 deficit of some $80 billion. The United States' comfortable control as the sole producer in entire sectors of the marketplace has been eroded to the point where almost any market in which it has primacy will immediately be taken over by one of its friendly competitors if it interrupts its production and sale through strikes, trade embargoes, or simple corporate mismanagement. In short, fungibility, which was originally used to describe the world grain market, has now become a fact of life in virtually all trade in the world.

These basic factors should be kept in mind when addressing the more narrow and prosaic questions that corporations consider as they approach a business relationship with an adversary country. The gradations in what is meant by adversary, the diminishing domination by U.S. corporations of the international marketplace, and the internationalization of production have dramatically changed what had been a fairly simple picture.

## VIEWING BUSINESS OPPORTUNITIES

What is it that a corporation looks at when it views a business opportunity in the Soviet Union or in another so-called adversary state? First and foremost, the corporation must determine whether it can properly develop a business relationship with the country in question that is consistent with the national interest of the United States and that the corporation can defend publicly as being in the national interest (or at least not damaging to the national interest) while being profitable to the corporation. The degree of sophistication in the U.S. business community has grown tremendously in this respect since World War II. The attitude in the United States in the early postwar era was perhaps typified by the incredible story of a major U.S. tire manufacturer that withdrew from a joint venture with Romania in the 1950s because political activists had gone to the nation's gas stations with posters declaring that tires made by company X should be boycotted because company X was working for the communists. That perception of the United States' relationship with the countries of Eastern Europe is hard to believe today, given the national recognition that some of Washington's truest allies are the hostage peoples of Eastern Europe. Many people now believe that the more the United States can strengthen its ties with those peoples through trade, the looser Moscow's hold will become.

The second most important factor for businesses interested in East-West trade is the predictability of the relationship. Businesses want to know whether it is possible to initiate a business relationship that will survive over several years. The start-up costs far outweigh the average annual profit and, in almost any product line, a trade relationship makes good sense only if it can be sustained over several years. Secretary of State George Shultz, in an earlier incarnation, wrote a widely quoted piece about "lightswitch diplomacy," emphasizing that predictability is absolutely essential for U.S. corporations if they are to trade competitively in the international marketplace.

A major concern of businesses, of course, is the question of profitability. Before World War II, profitability also was a fairly simple notion. Anything the corporation sold overseas had to realize a 20 to 50 percent profit margin to cover the perceived cost of doing international business. Today, the concept of profitability is much more complicated. Firms have learned the hard way, particularly in the last five years as the full impact of the OPEC energy revolution has taken hold, that profit considerations must include the capacity of a potential trading partner to finance, fund, and support the project or business deal under consideration. Corporations must look to the International Monetary Fund, Export-Import Bank, World Bank, and Agency for International Development as well as to the more mundane and simple question of, "Can we make a profit on this product?" They have to know that they can make a profit, that the host can pay the cost, and that conditions will permit the host to continue paying that price in the future.

Another rather amorphous concept, which corporations ignore or underestimate at their own peril, is market growth potential. This is not a simple question. The treacherous territory of market assessments in the United States is amplified many times over by the imponderables of the international marketplace, particularly when one deals in adversary states. In Marxist states (and other totalitarian states), the ability of the government to intervene arbitrarily with a political decision to discontinue a project launched by a U.S. corporation poses a continuing threat.

The potential for international competition is also an important consideration for businesses interested in trading with adversaries. Grinding ball plants in Chile, enjoying sole supply advantages, will be highly profitable. A similar ammonia fertilizer project in the Soviet Union may seem assured of profit, but woe to the corporation that ignores the Belgian competitor who can quickly render noncompetitive what seemed a guaranteed project. It is essential, therefore, to assess the potential for international competition very carefully. Once again, in dealing with so-called adversary states, the appearance of a foreign competitor can often be the result of a political decision by the adversary customer; this is an entirely new element in the international marketplace.

An increasing challenge to American corporations looking at potential business with adversary states is the balance between product sales and the capacity to produce. The questions that dominate business deals with China today, for example, are the sale of technology, the construction of turnkey plants, and the training of employees. The old central themes—groping with the administrative hassle of doing business in a hostile environment, coping with a suspicious and particularly difficult customs service, and the inability to provide U.S. technicians and business managers with a minimum standard of living—are all dwarfed in significance these days by the problems mentioned above. They do, however, remain serious disadvantages that U.S. corporations continue to consider as they look at potential trade with adversaries.

THE FAILURE OF CONTROLS

The current congressional debate about the renewal of the Export Administration Act is an interesting case study of U.S. understanding of its adversaries. Two events created an unusual consensus (virtually unanimous) among the business community in the country and changed congressional attitudes in a historic fashion. The Carter administration's awkward and ineffective reaction to the Soviet invasion of Afghanistan created a dramatic crisis in the agricultural sector of the United States. Not only did President Carter's grain embargo fail to have any significant impact on Soviet consumers or the Soviet economy, it was extremely expensive to American farmers and to the wide-ranging business community that supports the agricultural sector. The embargo affected grain prices, disrupted the use of grain rail cars, and seriously distorted the traditional patterns in grain storage, silo rental, farm mortgages, agricultural equipment needs, river barge traffic, and so on. Leaders of the agricultural community, including farm state representatives in the Senate and the House of Representatives, agreed that by

the end of 1982 the cumulative costs to the American agricultural sector exceeded $40 billion.

Notwithstanding the recently renewed U.S.-Soviet grain
agreement, the cost of the embargo is, to a large extent,
permanent. Prior to the grain embargo, U.S. farmers held
almost 80 percent of the Soviet grain import market. Today
that figure is closer to 30 percent. The main beneficiary
of the embargo was Argentina, which was provided with a sound
financial basis to invest in port modernization, rail transportation, and increased grain plantings and which has become a major grain exporter for the first time. Canada and
Western Europe also benefited, and the amount of grain imported by the Soviet Union was virtually unchanged. It was
only the U.S. participation in that market that changed dramatically.

The second event was the politically dramatic oil-gas
pipeline sanction crisis. In response to the brutal suppression of Solidarity by Polish police backed with implied
Soviet force, the Reagan administration ended all U.S. participation in the major oil-gas pipeline project from the
Soviet Union to the Western European energy marketplace. The
President not only cut off direct U.S. participation but
also attempted to block participation by Western European
companies holding U.S. licenses. This debate splintered
NATO as had no other political crisis since the alliance's
formation. Bitter exchanges between Washington and European
capitals were the order of the day. Great Britain passed
legislation that penalized American or British firms for
participating in the American embargo action. Finally, following the arrival of the experienced international business-
man, George Shultz, at the helm of the Department of State,
the administration retreated. The principal losers from the
sanctions were the American suppliers.

These two events unified the business community and
alarmed those in Congress who finally awoke to the fact that
unilateral trade sanctions may make one feel good for the
moment but are extremely costly to U.S. interests and to the
strength of the alliance, while they penalize the target not
one whit. In its campaign to make the renewed Export Administration Act reflect these lessons, the business community
laid out five principal objectives:

1. There should be no unilateral export boycotts by the United States.
2. Contract sanctity must be respected.
3. There is no legal basis for extraterritorial controls over companies located in allied countries.
4. Foreign policy controls are of limited if any value and should only be imposed in concert with allies and with other more substantive initiatives in the defense and political fields.
5. Penalties for those who violate U.S. export regulations should be greatly strengthened to take care of 85 percent of the technology leaks claimed by the Department of Defense since World War II.

Partly as a result of this, the Export Administration Act renewal has been the product of two bills, one House and one Senate, both of which attack the problems highlighted by the newly unified business community. They both recognize the global nature of the world economy and the fungibility of technology and industrial products, and they ensure that any new legislation will go a long way to meet the principal objectives of the business alliance.


CONCLUSION

It is important to recognize that no significant U.S. corportion will wittingly "sell the rope with which the Soviets intend to hang us"--quite the contrary. Those U.S. corporations engaged in East-West trade believe on the whole that increased contact through trade contributes to efforts to break down the isolated dictatorial regimes faced by the United States. If one accepts, as most people do, that nuclear war must not be inevitable and nuclear confrontation must gradually be reduced, then one must accept a policy of erosion rather than explosion of tension in confronting the Soviet Union. The inexorable historic process of economic interdependence is a strong instrument with which to accomplish this. If that process is synchronized and monitored properly through a strong cooperative effort, it can be the most effective policy to advance the U.S. national interest and the interests of the free world in breaking down the objectionable and threatening aspects of adversaries.

Most U.S. business executives engaged in East-West trade believe that stimulating consumerism in the Soviet Union and Eastern Europe produces pressures within the Soviet economy and Soviet society that are positive and in the U.S. national interest. These same executives and most career specialists in Soviet affairs agree that increased personal contact and exchanges with Soviet managers and decisionmakers in the economic process produces an infectious result that, in the long run--and the long run must be emphasized--can only be advantageous to the United States. This view is shared by most corporate leaders who, after all, are among the more conservative members of U.S. society. They believe that a strong defense shield with a seductive economic counteroption is the best combination to have in the United States' posture toward its adversaries.

Some business executives occasionally may serve Soviet propaganda goals through naiveté or gratuitous praise; the Reverend Billy Graham's recent performance in Moscow comes to mind more easily than that of any business representative, but certainly the late Cyrus Eaton was an example from the business world. With very few exceptions, the majority of business leaders who have pursued business relationships in the Soviet Union and other adversary countries are hard-nosed, sophisticated, and determined to proceed only when it is in the best interests of the United States. Traditionally, they continually touch base with the Department of State and the Department of Commerce to review what they are doing. They are very receptive to any recommendations to go slow, back off, or back out of individual projects. Many of them have extensive first-hand negotiating experience with the Soviets and appreciate only too well the seamy aspects of Soviet power. In short, one has to be impressed and comfortable with the judgment of the business community in its approach to doing business with its adversaries.

# 7

# THE POLITICS OF TRADE WITH ADVERSARIES

## Neil C. Livingstone

This chapter opens with a word about myth making.
Most people think of myths as larger-than-life tales of her-
oism and the whims of the gods--the product, in short, of
primitive minds. Yet myths are very much a part of the civilized mind as well. The myths of the cultured mind are
simply more complex, more sophisticated, but in many respects no less entrenched in our consciousness than the
myths that govern the rhythms and folkways of primitive society. Many people today embrace myths with an extraordinary passion despite ample evidence of their falseness, and
sometimes are even angry when the myths are debunked.

In this connection, politics is largely a myth-making
process, and political myth making is rarely more apparent
than in the realm of international trade. This is attributable, in part, to the megavariable nature of international
economics. The study of international economics is a decidedly inexact science, and this "comprehension gap" often
encourages axiomatic responses to unique situations, in
disregard of the harsh lessons of experience.

Many of the political and economic developments of
the twentieth century have augured for a truly global free-
market economy. Crisis after crisis points out the need to
exploit comparative advantages permitting maximum efficiency
in terms of global economic goals, including the development
of the nonindustrialized nations of the Third World and a

closing of the gap between the Northern and Southern Hemi-
spheres, the "haves" and the "have nots."

One of the most pervasive myths of the contemporary
world, the product of more wishful thinking than hard facts,
is that international trade can exist in a value-free environment, apart from political imperatives and passions.
Those who hold this view maintain that the world is an economic universe marked off by vectors of supply and demand
rather than borders and gunboats. As experience teaches us,
however, virtually every form of human endeavor has a political dimension, and when politics is injected into anything,
even the simplest economic truths often cease to be simple.
As Richard J. Barnet has observed, "Once demystified, the
dismal science [economics] is nothing less than the study of
power," and hence inseparable from politics. Accordingly,
with respect to international trade, politics will always be
primary, economic laws secondary. Mindful of this reality,
the goal should be to minimize distortions of the international marketplace caused by politics. Thus, one arrives
at the problem of political adversaries as potential trading
partners.

An adversary is most often defined as a nation that
has failed what is often referred to as the "McCarthy Test,"
after Joseph rather than Eugene. But even in obvious cases,
distinctions and labels have a tendency to blur. In many
respects, it is often much easier to trade with an adversary
such as Czechoslovakia or Hungary than an ally such as Japan.
And the problem of how to categorize Iran, or for that matter France, is a challenging one.

Another imposing question is, Should the United States
trade freely with the enemies of our allies? How does one
reconcile, for example, this nation's ongoing support for
Israel with our lucrative trade with the Arab world, including nations such as Libya, which borders on being an outlaw
nation. From the standpoint of political purists, there
would seem to be a clash of principle and profit here.

In the best of worlds, politics and economics are separate and distinct disciplines, whose theories and practices
should be kept as separate as church and state. Yet, the
fact remains--and here, as Shakespeare would say, "is the
rub"--some of the United States' political enemies include
some of its most promising trade partners, and the value of

their commerce must be considered in terms of United States' national security and considerations of the values that U.S. society holds dear.

This said, a second myth to be debunked is that trade sanctions are an effective tool of international politics. In matter of fact, trade sanctions are notoriously ineffective. This conclusion is consistently supported by history, dating--in terms of the United States' own national experience--from Jefferson's ill-considered embargo on British goods, which was a major contributing factor precipitating the War of 1812, down through President Roosevelt's embargo of scrap iron and steel to Japan prior to World War II. Indeed, the pursuit of trade with political adversaries finds backhanded support in a number of recent politically motivated trade actions, all of which have rebounded to the detriment of the United States.

Poland imposed martial law on its citizens in late 1981, and the United States responded by imposing economic sanctions on the already crippled Polish economy. The result of this action was, of course, negligible. It produced more disturbances in the U.S. economy than in the Polish economy and, while it may have scored a few symbolic points, it did nothing to temper the actions of either the Polish or Soviet governments.

An even better example is the Soviet invasion of Afghanistan. How did the United States express its considerable and absolutely justifiable outrage? It pulled out of the Olympic Games and imposed embargoes on grain and on the export of oil-drilling equipment and technology. The first acton was, again, purely symbolic, the second bruised our own farmers more than the Soviets, and the third created rancor between the United States and several of its major European allies, resulting in millions of dollars of lost sales to American manufacturers. These actions on the part of the Carter administration were surpassed for sheer futility only by Carter's suggestion that all Americans burn a candle in their front window to protest the invasion. The United States would have been far better off with a military rather than an economic response; that is, arm the Afghan rebels while selling wheat to Moscow. In other words, let the Soviets help pay for the Mujaheddin resistance effort. People often are reminded of Lenin's belief that the capitalists would sell socialism everything necessary for its triumph over capitalism. The flipside of the same coin is, Why not let the Soviets underwrite a war to defeat communism?

In other words, the United States should develop a two-tiered system involving, on the one hand, trade with its adversaries and, on the other hand, firmness in the face of Soviet aggression or other misbehavior on the part of the adversaries. Some would see this as inconsistent, but it is not. Military action should be parried with other military moves, not by taking bread away from the Soviet people, for that will have no practical impact on the USSR, where people have no real say in their government. The only thing the Soviets understand is force, and trade sanctions do not qualify as force.

Moreover, people in the United States labor under the myth that trade with adversaries benefits them more than it does us. Of course, it must be of equal benefit to both parties to have any real value or to be sustained by a base of support over time. A corollary to this myth is another myth, popular in some quarters, that the United States can somehow control--like a spigot that can be turned on and off--the flow of technology from the West to communist adversaries. Without the full and absolute cooperation of all of the industrialized nations of the West, which in the past has been unattainable, there is no effective means to keep the Soviets and their allies from acquiring mainstream Western technology. If denied certain technology by the United States, all the Soviets have to do under most circumstances is to approach France, West Germany, or Japan, and chances are they will be successful. Thus, the iron law of trade sanctions--boycotts, embargoes, and export controls-- only works if everyone who matters subscribes to them. As Undersecretary Olmer observed, controls, in order to be effective, must be multilateral in character.

This is not to suggest that the United States should blindly embrace its enemies. Genuine national security concerns must take precedence over possible economic gains. The United States should not export high technology with primary defense implications, or anything else that will cause irreparable harm to its national interest. As President Dwight D. Eisenhower admonished, "Don't sell them anything they can throw back at us." Furthermore, any nation seeking to obtain defense technology or high-technology material illegally from domestic sources should be subjected to the stiffest possible sanctions, including cutting off all trade.

A further difficulty involved in trading with political adversaries is that domestic pressures and political passions often spill over into the international arena and distort trade flows, even <u>before</u> legitimate national security concerns are taken into account. Human rights issues such as Soviet restrictions on Jewish emigration can disrupt and constrain trade despite the absence of any national security dimension. In the same sense, unemployment in the U.S. domestic textile industry is one of China's toughest political problems, and U.S. trade officials and lawmakers who ignore the political impact of unemployment do so at their own peril.

As Dr. Czinkota wrote in his introductory remarks, there is a need to build a national consensus. In this regard, it is easy enough to see how a well-managed public relations effort can help defuse the political tensions inherent in developing trade links with adversaries. In this connection, good public relations is the bedrock on which international agreements are built, be it the sale of grain to the Soviet Union or the SALT II treaty. Good public relations is the essential element in coalition building, which is, in the final analysis, the way to get anything done: to create a groundswell of popular support behind a given policy or action. Few policymakers are ever willing to get too far out in front of their constituents, but most are willing to lead a popular movement.

To this end, those responsible for trade policy must start with the assumption that trade is mutually desirable and build their argument on that foundation. The United States' willingness to trade with its political adversaries should be seen as a testmonial to its self-confidence and the superiority of its economic system. After this, it becomes a matter of enlisting allies. By making clear the mutually beneficial aspects of a trade relationship--which to a western wheat farmer is not too difficult to do--in as many influential public forums as possible, one can begin to shape opinion and build a solid base of support.

Identifying and drafting third-party beneficiaries to support the cause is a necessary but exacting, and sometimes exasperating, process. The outrage everyone feels over an action as senseless and barbaric as the downing of the Korean jetliner can sometimes blind even the most ardent capitalist to a bright opportunity. Though not an adversary situation, one is reminded of the effort undertaken by those who supported the Lockheed loan guarantee to secure its approval by the Congress. A thorough breakdown as to where every single nut and bolt of every single Lockheed product was manufactured was fed into a computer, subcontractors and suppliers were identified, and every service company, transport company, and other beneficiary was catalogued. Ultimately it became possible to isolate every last job in the United States that depended on Lockheed's survival and to pinpoint its location. Then and only then was it an easy matter to walk into a Senator or Congressman's office and explain the economic impact that Lockheed's failure would have on his constituents. Even a well-known and vocal "dove" such as former Senator George McGovern changed his mind and voted for the loan guarantee when educated as to the ripple effect that Lockheed's failure would produce in his state of South Dakota. A similar lobbying strategy was adopted by Boeing during the AWACS debate and by the Japanese during the local content struggle, wherein U.S. dealers of Japanese cars were enlisted to carry the battle to Washington. In the final analysis, the creation of trade lobbies to support individual trade agreements and sales is the only way to ensure that trade does not invariably become the handmaiden of politics.

Foreign governments, especially adversary governments, could be of more help in this process by showing greater understanding of and sensitivity to U.S. domestic political considerations. Many governments—probably a majority of this nation's trading partners—are characterized by an oversimplified and even naive understanding of the United States' political process. To illustrate this point, one need only to refer to the amazed consternation of the Canadian government at the Senate's refusal to ratify the 1979 East Coast Fisheries Treaty, in spite of the President's support. The United States' nearest neighbor and far and away largest trading partner has, it seems, never gotten a handle on the separation of powers. Next time they will know just how far it is from the White House to the Capitol.

The Reagan administration is to be applauded for the pragmatism that has guided it with respect to international trade. The elimination of the grain embargo, along with new assurances to the Soviets that neither "hell nor high water" would disrupt the agreement, is a positive step in recognizing the realities of the international marketplace. Moreover, the restraint demonstrated by the President following the Korean Air Lines incident has won Reagan approving marks all around the globe. An administration less secure in its knowledge of history and less sensitive to legitimate domestic political concerns might have felt compelled to slap a new--and equally ineffective--embargo on U.S. goods and products destined for the Soviet Union.

In summary, the economic goals touched on in this chapter are based on history, not some manifesto, and are grounded in pragmatism, rather than politics. Free trade, after all, has no ideology; it is a road that any country can take without prejudicing its form of government or the character and content of its politics. The first tenet of this philosophy is that "you don't have to love them or even like them to do business with them." The bottom line is that the benefits of trade with a particular adversary must outweigh the disadvantages. If this simple rule is adhered to, it should be relatively easy to build a constituency to support East-West trade.

Such a philosophy runs counter to many of the myths people have too often attempted to live by, because it is inherently rational rather than emotional and because it stems from an understanding of adversaries, not a blind fear of them. The particulars may change. Today's ally may be tomorrow's adversary, making today's investment tomorrow's write-off. However, the underlying principles that guide U.S. actions--those of free trade and a respect for the most fundamental human rights--are quite constant.

# 8

# THE DANGERS OF DEPENDENCE

## Miles M. Costick

Let me stress from the very beginning the nature of our analysis at the Institute on Strategic Trade. The accent is on strategic, and there is nothing in terms of historical precedence or empirical analysis to suggest that there is another element in the analysis of East-West commerce that would take precedence over the strategic considerations. East-West economic relations have been a process of policy and the policymakers are governments, as is logical. One cannot expect an individual commercial entity to determine either United States foreign policy or United States foreign economic policy. That is a prerogative of the government.

Economic detente as conceived by Henry Kissinger, according to his own definition, was a political proposition aimed at taming an unruly animal in the international arena. Today, however, according to Henry Kissinger, that policy must be considered a failure. In that respect, I would like to call your attention to the series of articles by Henry Kissinger on this subject in the Baltimore Sun and in Foreign Policy and to the speeches he gave on three continents, from Japan to Europe. Kissinger emphasized that the policy of economic detente--in terms of his basic conception--was a failure. If one looks at Soviet behavior during the past 12 years--their relentless military build-up and aggression in various forms around the world--one can recognize that economic detente has failed. It has not tamed them. It has not civilized their behavior in accordance with some civil perception of international law.

The beginning of Western trade with the Soviet Union was rationalized by England's former Prime Minister Lloyd George, who said, "I believe we can save her [Soviet Russia] by trade. Commerce has a sobering influence. . . . Trade, in my opinion, will bring an end to the ferocity, the rapine, and the crudity of Bolshevism surer than any other method."

The Soviets clearly have a different view. Lenin, for example, said: "One cannot be satisfied with the collapse of capitalism. It is necessary to take all its science, technology, etc. Without that we will not be able to build Communism." In May 1973, at a secret meeting of the leaders of the Warsaw Pact communist parties in Prague, Czechoslovakia, Leonid Brezhnev explained detente in the following words: "We communists have got to string along with the capitalists for a while. We need their credits, their agriculture and their technology, but we are going to continue massive military programs and by the middle 80s we will be in a position to return to a much more aggressive foreign policy designed to gain the upper hand in our relationship with the West." And on February 3, 1952, the Soviet delegate to the United Nations, Yaakov Malik had said in the presence of the delegates of all other countries, "World War III has, in fact, begun."

If one takes a scrutinizing look at the West's communist trading partners, one sees that the West faces economies that are basically autarkic. Furthermore, in the case of the Soviet Union, the government has a monopsonistic position and conducts its economic affairs on the basis of political, strategic, and ideological considerations. There is no economic rationale in terms of traditional Anglo-Saxon economic thought. The conduct is primarily in accordance with the definition of the purpose of Soviet economy given by Lenin, who said, "The purpose or objective of the Soviet economy is to facilitate the might of the Soviet state."

From that position, the USSR conducts its economic affairs within the country and outside the country. Consequently, a General Electric or a General Motors does not deal with an individual economic entity in the Soviet Union,

but with the entire might of the Soviet state.  As a result,
these companies pale into insignificance despite their size.
The free-world firms are subject to whipsawing and other
unfair methods that a totalitarian state--committed to the
destruction of the free-market economies--routinely
practices.

Of the research and development in the Soviet Union
conducted by the institutes of the Soviet Academy of
Science, 80 percent is for the military establishment,
which is represented by the 12 ministries that comprise the
Soviet military-industrial complex.  There is not a single
factory in the Soviet Union that does not produce for the
military.  The factories in the military-industrial complex
produce about 80 percent for the military and the rest, after
being rejected by military commissions, goes into consumer
products.

It would be interesting to see what a relative contemporary from Soviet officialdom had to say about the conduct of Soviet foreign economic policy and its purposes.
When Henry Kissinger spoke about linkage between trade and
Soviet conduct, the Soviets rejected the concept on numerous
occasions, publicly and in meetings with U.S. representatives.  In the spring of 1978, however, Soviet Prime Minister Alexei Kosygin put the major Soviet trading partners
on notice that the Soviet Union intended to link its economic relationships with them to their foreign policy conduct; their foreign policy had to be acceptable to the
Soviet Union as far as key international issues were concerned.  Kosygin's speech appeared in _Pravda_, the organ of
the Soviet communist party, on March 2, 1978, as a warning
that the Soviet Union intended to tie Soviet foreign economic policy to the behavior of other nations on unrelated
military and political matters.

This Soviet statement should be compared with a Soviet
insistence, over time, particularly marked in its dealings
with the United States, that linkage between trade and political questions is impermissible.  Now let me quote Kosygin's
statement:

> In trade and other international exchanges, we
> see an effective means of enhancing detente and
> trust between states.  At the same time, every-

thing that undermines trust cannot promote international trade either. This means first and
foremost a build-up of military preparations,
interference in the affairs of other people, and
encouragement, in particular by armed supplies,
of the peace-endangering course of those forces
pursuing the policy of expansionism and subver-
sion of international detente. All of this cannot but cloud prospects for economic links with
relevant countries, and we shall to an even
greater extent orient ourselves to cooperation
with those who do not jeopardize long-term
interests for the sake of dubious benefits in
the immediate situations.

The prime and immediate target of this signal by a
Soviet official was the German Federal Republic. The particular focus was and is on the ongoing debate in that
country over whether to go along with the replacement of
short-range Pershing I nuclear missiles with Pershing II
and cruise missiles capable of reaching the Soviet Union.
This debate, according to the Soviet publication Life Abroad
on February 22, 1979, involves a struggle between two distinct lines: one favoring better relations with the Soviet
Union and the other focusing on the deterrent strategy in
the face of an alleged Soviet military threat to Western
Europe.
    On December 5, 1979, Izvestia, the Soviet government's
news organ, stated: "Trade, industrial and technical ties
are a substantial and essential component of Soviet-West
German relations." And, in June of 1983, Soviet Colonel
General Nikolay Chervov, discussing the motives for West
Germany's Ostpolitik policy of detente with the Soviet Union
in a Hungarian television interview, said,

This policy is . . . determined not so much by
who is in power in Bonn, but far more by West
Germany's real geopolitical position. . . .
This government will also continue the Ostpolitik. It cannot have another policy. This
policy is determined partly by economic interests, but there are also important political

factors.  After all, West Germany is still concerned with the long-term perspective of a
future unified Germany.  This problem . . .
cannot be solved without maintaining good relations with the USSR.

The Federal Republic of Germany is the number one
Soviet trading partner, with two-way exchanges over the past
ten years averaging $4 billion per year.  Obviously,
Kosygin's threat would not involve general cutbacks in
trade--which would be a dual-edged sword--but rather selective actions, such as a cutoff of energy supplies, an area
in which the USSR already occupies a critical position as
the German supplier.  Currently, imports of Soviet natural
gas run about 19 percent of total consumption in West
Germany; the import of Soviet petroleum accounts for about
9 percent of domestic consumption; and imports of enriched
uranium for nuclear power plants supply about 37 percent of
total West German needs.  If one evaluates German energy
dependence, one has to look at all components of it, including coal.  In 1978, the Soviet Union became a major supplier
of coal to West Germany, practicing the old custom of dump-
ing products on the West German market--namely, undersell-
ing coal in order to gain foreign currency and at the same
time undermining the position of the coal producers in
West Germany.
    If 40 percent of the West German specialty steel in-
dustry--actually the production of that industry--depends
on Soviet and other Council for Mutual Economic Assistance
(COMECON) markets, it is obvious that a prohibitively high
number of jobs depends on economic relationships with the
Soviet Union.  And since West German banks hold the majority
of IOUs of the Soviet bloc--the total of which, according
to my calculations (principle plus interest plus penalties),
stands at some $92 billion--it becomes obvious that the
German economy is, to a considerable extent, a captive of
its communist borrowers.  And the Soviets are skillfully
exploiting that for political and other purposes, not only
in Germany but also in Great Britain and other countries
to which large sums of money are owed.
    To cite an example of this, a major British bank,
which is heavily involved in financing Soviet bloc trade,

was approached by the Soviets and told: "You can't expect us to pay back unless we make some money; we are interested in acquiring a certain firm, and we need your help." And they got the help. The Soviets, with London Bank's help, lent £2 million to a British firm, Cylinder Forgings, an ammunitions manufacturer with contracts in France, Belgium, and the United Kingdom Ministry of Defence. The Cylinder Forgings firm was in financial trouble, and the Soviets exploited it in order to gain access to NATO secrets. The Moscow Narodny Bank had called in the receiver to the British firm. It dismissed the staff of Cylinder Forgings and closed the company, knowing it would lose almost all of its investment. Why? Simply because the company files contained secrets. Among NATO contracts on which Cylinder Forgings was working when it ceased trading was research work on the rocket engine of a new missile, details of which were classified and which fell into Soviet hands.

The use of trade as a weapon is not a new proposition to us. In our judgment, however, the utilization of sanctions clearly demonstrates that sanctions represent a cosmetic solution to the problem. The Soviets could teach us a lesson or two about the conduct of economic warfare. Before I discuss this further, I would like to stress one thing. The free world is faced with a global challenge, and there is no way to deal with a global challenge on a marginal basis. The global challenge requires a response that must include the economic component. We have to understand that an economic weapon is a weapon. In terms of security, it is beneficial. In terms of economic considerations, there are costs involved. But there is nothing important in our lives that does not entail costs.

If we are to survive as free people, we have no other alternative but to use our strength prudently. Instead of playing the game of cosmetic sanctions, we should use our economic and other related assets (such as science) in a long-term economic strategy against our self-declared communist adversaries, who are dedicated to the destruction of everything that the United States and all free peoples stand for. The major objective of U.S. long-term economic strategy vis-à-vis the Soviet Union should be to retard its scientific, technological, and economic progress. Only if we achieve this objective can we expect to continue to live as free people and to prosper.

# 9

# REALISM IN TRADE WITH ADVERSARIES

## John F. Dealy

In contrast to what has been written in other chapters about U.S. business conditions, this author's area of expertise and focus--high technology (microelectronics, information transfer, biotechnology)--is a vibrant, entrepreneurial-driven sector of the economy with high growth, high profits, tremendous domestic markets, and a very strong international position. People in high technology, though, are concerned about what may occur in the foreign trade area, specifically with regard to export controls, and their view might be worth examining.

Fundamentally, in discussing the development of a constructive program of trade with adversaries, the issue that this country has to come to grips with is not whether to play the game of international trade on a level playing field, but whether it is prepared to play at all. Some of the authors in other chapters, while using the polite words of diplomats, were in essence saying: "For foreign policy reasons or any other reasons at any time, we want to reserve the right not to play." Now, if one assumes the vantage point of a business executive--an executive making investment plans, projecting market penetrations, and analyzing growth prospects--a situation in which the government has said, "we will reserve the right not to play, and we are not even going to tell you when," is a very difficult environment in which to make aggressive investments. This uncertainty is what concerns leaders in technology when they sort through the verbiage and address the underlying concept of the government's position.

The second area that is very important for people to focus on when they discuss technology is the dramatic change in relative economic power among countries since World War II. In fact, it would be useful if the pertinent people in our government focused on this item. This is no longer a world where the United States holds all the cards, where we have all the technology, where others are waiting for us to confer some benefit or remove or exact some penalty when they do something we dislike. This is a world that has matured significantly, in which many other nations vie effectively with the United States in the market place.

Another central point is that this country's demographics have changed. It does not have the long-term domestic markets necessary to sustain the type of growth it has known historically. As a consequence, there has been a building of consensus, at least among the business community, academics, some members of Congress, and even parts of the Reagan administration——although here it gets overwhelmed by certain foreign policy issues——that the true issue facing this country is U.S. competitiveness in a world market over time, over some considerable period of time.

In viewing the issue of U.S. competitiveness, this country should look at what happened to the U.S. auto industry when it thought the only competition was among three or four domestic car makers. Or one could look at some other industries that deferred capital investment for years when they were earning high profits because they did not understand the world competitive environment they were ultimately going to have to face.

When one examines trade with adversaries, one should put the issue in the larger picture of where trade really stands in the view of the administration and in the view of business executives and policymakers in this country. It is clear that while trade is becoming more important, while it is a higher priority than it used to be, it is still not at the priority level that it should be in the deliberations within the Reagan administration and before the Congress. And that attitude is what poses the greatest long-term potential danger to effective trading relationships and U.S. competitiveness.

When one gets to the specific problem of trading with adversaries, one's views depend fundamentally on one's perspective and perception at a given time.  People are deeply committed to beliefs.  These beliefs often are not based on facts; instead, they may be based on a view of the world, on an ideology, on anger, on frustration.  This country has spent 35 years trying to deal with its political adversaries and has done so ineffectively.  The United States does not go through its motions and activities in Central America because it wants to play in Central America, but because it is unhappy about something that happened in Europe, or about some activity occurring in the Soviet Union, where we are powerless to act.  The same thing is true when Washington imposes export controls or changes trade rules to "slap wrists."  It is taking those actions out of frustration, and the remedy has nothing to do with the problem.

If one takes the different players in the system and looks at how they view the issue of trade with adversaries, it becomes clear that they have dramatically different positions.  When business people look at trade, even with the Soviet Union and the communist world, they really look for two things.  They are narrow and selfish--they want protection from foreign targeting.  Why?  Because they are trying to protect their own business and move out against the competition.  But, they also have a broader view, and that is they want stimulation of exports.  They do not see the communist world as a threat, they see it as a market.  It is small today, perhaps large tomorrow.

The Defense Department is more candid than most.  It notes, realistically, that sales to communist countries are not material to current U.S. business growth and survival.  In the view of Defense officials, communist countries use our goods to avoid investment they would otherwise have to make.  They then confound our military security by using their resources to offset our capabilities.  Our trade with them frees funds for anti-American mischief around the world.  As a consequence, the Defense Department regards any trade with the communist world as a threat, not a market.  Their view is the reverse of the business perspective.

State Department officials, on the other hand, do not see trade with communist countries as either a threat or a market.  State is also fairly realistic.  State officials

believe trade policy in the United States is and should be
subsidiary to foreign policy strategies. Why wouldn't they
say that? After all, they are the Department of State.
State says trade is an opportunity to achieve other goals,
to send signals, tighten alliances, loosen relationships,
and so on.

Washington's allies have a distinctly different view,
and this country would move more constructively in the area
of East-West trade if, as opposed to Ambassador Brock's suggestion that we communicate--whatever that means--with the
allies, we tried listening to them. There is a very good
book on negotiation by Harvard Professor Roger Fisher, who
was brought in on the Iranian hostage crisis, called Getting
to Yes. It says that in order to negotiate, particularly
with friends, one has to listen and try to understand their
position. One does not just communicate, which is a one-way
information dump, and wait for an agreement. It is not going
to happen.

What do the allies really see in terms of trade with
communist countries? Trade with the communist countries,
realistically for them, is both a market and a threat. The
market potential to the allies outweighs the threat for many
reasons, including years of contiguous living and interdependence in their societies. The allies believe they have to
coexist with their land and sea neighbors and that interdependence is on balance good if they are careful. Most people,
if they thought about it objectively, would probably come to
a similar conclusion. Interdependence between two adversaries who have, for whatever reason, decided not to come to
the ultimate confrontation should, over time, lead to more
constructive results than endlessly building walls and polar-
izing positions.

There are a few conclusions that can be made based on
these assertions. As mentioned before, trade is not a high
priority of this government. It is a priority higher than
it was in the last administration, but it is not of equal
priority with other issues. This is due, in part, to the
fact that this country still does not perceive the importance of trade in both directions to the long-term growth of
the U.S. economy. One can see this lack of perception in
the language in this book, from most of the authors, who
probably reflect the Reagan administration view. They talk
of trade in terms of a benefit to be conferred or a penalty

to be imposed. That simply is not what it is over time; trade is an interrelationship that is neither a benefit nor a penalty.

A second conclusion is that militarily significant technology should be controlled. The issues are how to define it and who polices it. If an item is not militarily significant, in the technological or intelligence sense, contracts should be honored and relations should be expanded. Threats have proved not to work. Removal of goods simply stimulates an indigenous economy to generate them or someone else to sell them.

The problem, when one looks at interdependence, is that it is always interdependence compared to what. The system this country now has with the communist countries certainly has not been very beneficial to us. Some limited form of interdependence would hardly be worse. When one looks at the kind of technology that the world is moving into--technology based on the microprocessor chip or based on small semiconductors that are rapidly being reduced in cost and complexity, and that are being manufactured in the four corners of the world--our concepts of control are unworkable. The technology is rapidly becoming ubiquitous, low cost, and very compact.

The government can write the rules, it can set up an army of people to check packages, it can do whatever it wants. But the technology that this country is developing--microprocessor-driven control systems and small chips with tremendous memory and computing capability--is not going to be controlled by bureaucratic systems. We had better recognize that. Ambassador Brock made the point that once something is on the shelf, in his view, it is obsolete. If that simple rule were adopted, there would be very few problems in export controls, because most of the items that are being discussed can be bought in a stereo store and put in a sound system, yet some people do not want them shipped to the Soviet Union. Moreover, much of this technology is available elsewhere, and that fact should be taken into account.

There are probably not any clear solutions to these problems because, for the moment, this country has elected not to play. If the United States does want to play, it must reexamine the importance of trade to its growth. With one in six American jobs dependent on trade, the United States has an enormous comparative advantage. It has a head start, brain power, and the greatest collection of entrepreneurial capital in the world. It has the markets to support the growth. This

country has all the resources necessary to dominate the
world in various high-technology areas. It will lose nothing
if the technology is disseminated to a few other countries;
it will get there very shortly anyway.

There is a need for a Department of Trade. The reason
for the department, though, is not that it is going to change
people's perceptions overnight, but that it will bring trade
issues up to the level where someone at the cabinet level
can debate them with someone else during policy decisions.

The United States should develop a view of the role of
trade more consistent with that of its allies. U.S. leaders
have to recognize that the allies have an interest in this,
and there has to be a way to meet them somewhere in the middle. The United States should develop a program of managed
interdependence, with contingency plans when things go wrong,
worked out with its allies. To have people as allies, one
has to have some respect for their judgments and some willingness to compromise.

We should define very narrowly any items to be on a
militarily critical technologies list, otherwise the door on
that technology for transfer will be shut.

The United States should try to remove trade as an instrument of foreign policy. This probably will never happen,
but the debate should continue. Is it effective to give and
take on trade, or even to use the club of withholding as an
instrument of foreign policy? We are the ones, remember,
who make trade the moral issue. Many other nations that
have been dependent on trade for a fundamental part of their
economies do not see it as a moral issue. In part, this is
because they do not begin by viewing trade as some large benefit that they are conferring on the trading partner.

As others have said, the United States should be more
discriminating among the Soviet Union, its allies, and other
communist countries, and it should craft a policy appropriate
for each. Certainly there has been some work done in that area.

Finally, the United States needs a clear understanding
of any issues regarding extraterritorial jurisdiction or
sanctity of contracts with our allies; we have to do that before a problem arises.

Taking these steps will not resolve all of the problems involved in export controls, but they are a start, a
framework with which this country can work.

# III

# THE IMPLEMENTATION AND
# EFFECT OF TRADE CONTROLS

Part III examines the effect of U.S. export control policy on businesses and foreign policy, and it discusses the problems encountered when controls are implemented. The section focuses on the effect of the U.S. imposition of sanctions against companies involved in the Soviet gas pipeline, and it provides useful information on the practical effects of U.S. policy.

Joseph E. Pattison examines one of the most pressing issues involved in export controls: the problem of extraterritorial enforcement of controls. In his chapter, Pattison looks at the international legal perspective on extraterritorial enforcement, using the recent pipeline controversy as his main example. Pattison argues that the imposition of extraterritorial jurisdiction did not have the backing of international law, and he points out that the imposition caused grievous political problems within NATO as well.

David H. Buswell explains how the pipeline sanctions affected his company, Fiatallis North America, Inc. According to Buswell, the U.S. sanctions were unnecessarily restrictive and caused Fiatallis to lose millions of dollars. He notes that the U.S. controls restricted Fiatallis's trade with the Soviet Union, causing a decline in company business and contributing to drastic cuts in employment. Buswell concludes by expressing the frustration of business executives who lost contracts only to see the damaging sanctions lifted after failure.

Stanley D. Nollen examines the effects the pipeline sanctions had on the British company John Brown Engineering Limited. He describes John Brown Engineering's business, then narrates the events of the pipeline controversy. Following this, Nollen examines the various options the British firm had open to it after sanctions were imposed against it, and he discovers that the firm was placed in the impossible position of receiving contradictory orders from the U.S. and British governments. He concludes by investigating the steps taken by the firm and concludes with some policy and business policy lessons learned.

The final chapter in the section is by Leonard Santos. Santos discusses the implementation of trade sanctions from his position in the U.S. Congress. In his discussion, which focuses on the implementation of the pipeline sanctions, Santos argues that little consideration was given to the costs of the sanctions to businesses such as Fiatallis and John Brown Engineering. He also argues that sanctions have become, by and large, an exercise in symbolism used by governments unwilling to impose harsher punishments for acts they disagree with. Santos concludes with a discussion of possible ways to improve the implementation of trade sanctions.

# 10

# EXTRATERRITORIAL ENFORCEMENT OF THE EXPORT ADMINISTRATION ACT

## Joseph E. Pattison

Some may wonder how anyone could possibly need an entire chapter to explain the views of commercial profit-
seeking interests on U.S. embargoes and other export controls. Most business executives would not need much time at
all to express their views on the subject since they feel
about such controls the same way they feel about jumping in
front of runaway locomotives or sleeping in trash compactors.
They would be much healthier without them. All told, such
controls are an experience they would rather avoid.

Unfortunately, the commercial problems posed by export
restrictions often cannot be avoided. They seem like very
painful salt in already existing wounds when added to the
export disincentives already built into America's antiboycott,
foreign corrupt practice, antitrust, and other laws, but during the last few years, American business executives have
had to develop a high threshold for such pain.

The heaviest dose of such salt in recent times was, of
course, the June 1982 imposition of expanded controls over
U.S. oil and gas equipment sold to the Soviet Union, controls more popularly known as the pipeline embargo. This
chapter focuses on the commercial ramifications of that embargo and similar measures and also explores their ramifica-
tion under international law.

When President Reagan announced, as part of the administration's response to repression in Poland, the implementation of the pipeline embargo, he launched a storm of criti-

cism and outrage in capitals throughout the world.[1] The
French Foreign Minister cited the measure as evidence of the
"progressive divorce" between the United States and Europe.[2]
West German Chancellor Helmut Schmidt stated publicly that
"by claiming the right to extend American laws to other countries [the U.S. embargo] is affecting not only the interests
of the European trade nations but also their sovereignty."[3]
In its formal comments on the expanded U.S. controls, the
European Economic Community argued that the new U.S. regulations contained "sweeping extensions of U.S. jurisdiction
which are unlawful under international law."[4] When he ordered four British companies to violate the controls by com-
plying with Soviet contracts, Lord Cockfield, England's Foreign Trade Secretary, formally announced that "the embargo
in the terms which it has been imposed is an attempt to interfere with existing contracts and is an unacceptable extension of American extraterritorial jurisdiction in a way that
is repugnant to international law."[5]

In short, the comments by other nations of the world,
including some of America's closest allies, were as negative
as they were loud. Critics in the United States were also
somewhat clamorous. One senior U.S. Senator, for example,
claimed that if the Kremlin itself had planned the pipeline
embargo, it could not have done a better job of uniting the
European allies against the United States. At the very least,
the pipeline controls gave new credence to Helmut Schmidt's
observation that being a U.S. ally is like being in a canoe
with an elephant.

Judging by those comments and the coverage they received in the press, one might reasonably conclude that the
United States had leapt into a totally uncharted and previously unexperienced realm of international relations. Unfortunately, the problems raised by the 1982 embargo were far
from a new phenomenon.

Indeed, such emphatic extraterritorial extensions, and
the furor they have raised in the capitals of our allies,
have seemed almost cyclical in recent years, rising and ebbing
with the changing tide of East-West relations.[6]

EXTRATERRITORIAL ENFORCEMENT THROUGH THE YEARS

In 1958, Canadian business executives adamantly pro-
tested U.S. foreign asset control regulations being applied

to block Canadian plans to sell a large number of motor vehicles to the People's Republic of China. Although Prime Minister Diefenbaker and President Eisenhower subsequently consulted to ease the resulting friction between the two countries, the U.S. action was of grave concern to its allies at that time.[7] Sixteen years later, when Canadian business executives thought such U.S. intervention was just a distant memory, the U.S. government discovered that Canada was contemplating the sale of 30 locomotives of U.S. content to Cuba and took similar blocking measures; the sale was carried out only after Prime Minister Trudeau conducted an intense lobbying campaign in Washington.[8] The U.S. government's continuing interest in controlling exports by American subsidiaries, licensees, or even customers located overseas was only underscored, however, when, in that same year, the U.S. Treasury Department moved to block an export license for the sale to Cuba of automobiles produced by a U.S. subsidiary in Argentina. Only after animated diplomatic exchanges did the United States agree, for the sake of "good relations with Argentina," to grant the license concerned.[9]

Nearly 20 years ago, a case involving Fruehauf–France, a 70 percent owned subsidiary of the Fruehauf Corporation, attracted a notoriety equivalent to the recent Dresser problem. When, in 1964, Fruehauf–France entered into a contract for the sale of truck trailers to a French truck manufacturer that intended to sell the final tractor trailer products to China, the U.S. Department of Treasury intervened in Fruehauf's Detroit headquarters. The Treasury Department warned Fruehauf that the proposed sale violated U.S. controls and that completion of the sale would result in the levying of severe criminal penalties against the U.S. parent company.[10] When the parent company ordered Fruehauf–France to cancel its contract, the French parties refused to accept what they perceived to be an unauthorized intervention in their business affairs. The French customer adamantly refused to release its supplier, threatening a $1 million lawsuit for breach of contract, and the three French directors of Fruehauf–France sued the subsidiary's U.S. directors in a French court to obtain appointment of a trustee to assume temporary control for execution of the contract.[11] As a result of this action by the French courts, the U.S. Department of Treasury argued that the subsidiary was no longer ruled by its U.S. parent

and therefore was not subject to U.S. jurisdiction for purposes of commercial controls. Washington and Fruehauf U.S.A.
washed their hands of the entire affair and the sale proceeded as planned.[12]

While the files of the Department of Commerce are re-
plete with cases involving other "long-arm" controls—including, for example, controls over the transshipment of goods
to restricted third countries—by far the most controversial
and destructive controls are restrictions placed on foreign
entities on the basis of some general U.S. connection.[13]
From both a commercial and a legal perspective, the most important question to be asked is whether the U.S. government
has the authority to extend its export controls to U.S.-
related entities in foreign countries.

The problems inherent in attempting to influence foreign subsidiaries through such measures are reflected in the
fact that in several recent embargoes, including those relating to the Moscow Olympics, Afghanistan, and Uganda, the
United States has refrained from seeking to control foreign
subsidiaries.[14] In the Iranian hostage case, however, the
President exercised the authority in the International Emergency Economic Powers Act to block Iranian assets possessed
or controlled by all persons subject to the jurisdiction of
the United States.[15] Although this action was triggered by
Iranian intent to withdraw certain government deposits from
the foreign branches of American banks, subsequent measures
applied to any person subject to the jurisdiction of the
United States but specifically exempted nonbanking entities
organized in foreign countries.

The pipeline embargo, which remained in force until
November 13, 1982, was, of course, the most recent extension
of U.S. export authority into foreign economies.[16] Several
foreign companies were involved, including those using American technology, such as Alsthome Atlantique, and those using
U.S. component products directly, such as John Brown Engineering of Great Britain.[17] At the time of the embargo imposition, it was estimated that U.S. companies would directly
lose $300 to $600 million in exports and that foreign subsidiaries and licensees would lose as much as $1.6 billion
as a result of these sanctions.

At the time of the expanded pipeline controls, the
wholly owned French subsidiary of Dresser Industries had en-

tered into a contract with a Soviet trading company and a
company controlled by the French government to supply and
manufacture compressors used for the transmission of natural
gas.  The only export as such used by Dresser-France in this
contract was U.S. technical data that had been exported from
the United States prior to 1981, when the first set of U.S.
pipeline sanctions was announced.[18]  Although Dresser-France
immediately stopped production due to the new U.S. controls,
it provided those products it had completed under the contract for shipment on a Soviet freighter.  When the Deputy
Assistant Secretary of Commerce for Export Enforcement
threatened sanctions should the compressors be loaded for
the Soviet Union, the French government threatened its own
sanctions if Dresser-France did not honor its contract.

Thus, being damned if they did ship and damned if they
did not ship, Dresser Industries and Dresser-France had no
choice but to file suit in the United States for declaratory
and injunctive relief.[19]  The court denied their claims and
refused to provide them latitude for completing the Soviet
shipment.  The U.S. Commerce Department proceeded to black-
list Dresser-France through a temporary denial order.[20]  This
order was modified on September 9, 1982, to permit Dresser-
France to obtain licensing for goods and data unrelated to
the exploration, transmission, or production of oil and
gas.[21]  The subsequent lifting of the pipeline export restrictions on November 13, 1982, effectively rendered these
actions moot.

The Dresser case underscored the need for clarification of the legal authority for such actions.  The pipeline
controls raised serious issues because of their retroactive
aspect, an element that West Germany seriously criticized.
In effect, the Commerce Department sought through the 1982
controls to control a transfer of technology that had been
legally completed at an earlier date.  Its controls worked
to divest property rights that came into existence at the
time of the legal export of Dresser technology to France,
effectively "taking" such property, in a legal sense, without
due process of law.  U.S. courts of law refuse to apply statutes and implementing regulations retroactively without a
pertinent, clear expression of congressional intent for such
retroactive impact, particularly in instances where antece-
dent rights are at stake.[22]  The Export Administration Act

provides no clear authorization of retroactive export controls,[23] but it does require the President, in implementing controls for foreign policy reasons, to consider:

> The likely effects of the proposed controls on the export performance of the United States . . . and on individual U.S. companies and their employees and communities, including the effects of the controls on the existing contracts.[24]

Such a directive falls short of the clear expression of retroactive intent required by courts.

## EXTRATERRITORIAL INTENT OF CONGRESS

By far the most important legal issue raised in the June 1982 order resulted from its reach into the internal economies of many European countries. It behooves not only the U.S. government but also any other entities significantly involved in foreign trade to determine exactly how far the government can reach to exert its policies through export controls. A fundamental principle of American jurisprudence is that the statutes of the United States apply only to conduct occurring within or having effects within the territory of the United States, subject only to exceptions that are clearly and forcefully stated by Congress.[25] This presumption against extraterritorial effects has been applied meticulously by the courts, which have found exceptions to it only in highly limited circumstances and generally only when clear legislative intent for extraterritorial application could be shown.[26] For example, it has been found that the United States has the authority, under pain of criminal contempt, to require the return of its citizens residing in foreign countries[27] or to extend bankruptcy laws to reach property that had been concealed overseas by American debtors.[28]

Although the preceding export statute contained no real expression of extraterritorial application,[29] Congress revised the laws in 1977 to permit the extension of export controls to any shipments "subject to the jurisdiction of the United States or exported by any person subject to the jurisdiction of the United States."[30] The legislative history of this amendment was to "confer non-emergency authority . . . to control non-U.S. origin exports by foreign subsidiaries of U.S. concerns." This language remained unchanged through the 1979 amendments to the act.

Indeed, the Senate expressly considered a proposal to prohibit U.S. export controls on foreign subsidiaries of U.S. companies. Despite allusions to past protests of American allies over entities ostensibly subject to their protection, the Senate refused to accept this revision and, by maintaining coverage of the act over any persons subject to the jurisdiction of the United States, it expressed the intention to control goods supplied by foreign U.S. subsidiaries.[32]

## THE INTERNATIONAL LAW PERSPECTIVE

Although the current export law extends by its own language to "any person subject to the jurisdiction of the United States, including extension to foreign entities somehow related to the United States," the U.S. legal system also has a firmly entrenched rule against construction of U.S. statutes in a manner that violates the laws of other nations and international law generally.[33] The importance of international and foreign law in the U.S. export control framework was underscored, moreover, in the pipeline controversy. The severe diplomatic tension that ultimately resulted in the cancellation of the June 1982 controls was essentially the result of complaints made by U.S. allies under international legal principles. The allies' perception that the June 1982 controls were blatantly illegal under those legal principles ultimately proved to be a cost that the Reagan administration could not afford to pay.[34] Indeed, if any lesson could have been learned from the pipeline embargo experience, it would certainly relate to the need for consideration of the international legal framework prior to imposition of such controls. While international law does not have the same impact in every country of the world, it nonetheless is sufficiently recognized by U.S. allies to give rise to major legal disputes when extraterritorial enforcement is sought by a member of the world community.[35]

Briefly speaking, what is the nature of the international legal framework into which U.S. export controls must fit? In essence, it is founded on the cardinal premise of international law that nations enjoy sovereign and equal status with rights of independence, national supremacy, and territorial supremacy.[36] Territorial supremacy for this purpose is the state's power to exercise "supreme authority" over all persons and things within its territory.[37] The territorial principle establishes that a state has absolute jurisdiction and control over all acts committed within its territory and all individuals and property located within its borders.[38] A state's territory is susceptible to no limitation not imposed by itself.[39]

Indeed, U.S. assertions of extraterritorial jurisdiction in its past enforcement of antitrust and other laws have led several European nations to protect their territorial supremacy by passing what are known as "blocking" statutes to protect their nationals from what is perceived as the overreaching of U.S. law enforcement.[40] Such laws, which generally block compliance with foreign directives for inspection of documents or compulsion of evidence for use in a foreign jurisdiction, are a direct result of U.S. antitrust enforcement efforts overseas. The British government was quick to use its blocking law in the pipeline case to order British companies to disregard the American controls or suffer substantial penalties under British law.[41]

An important corollary to the territorial principle is the duty of foreign states to refrain from acts that infringe on territorial supremacy.[42] Certain bodies within the international framework have held that attempts by one nation to enforce its own laws within another nation violate this duty.[43]

Of course, no rule of law affecting export trade would be complete without a number of exceptions. The most significant of these is the nationality principle, under which a country may impose its legal framework on its citizens anywhere in the world. The United States and other countries use this premise to enforce nearly all extraterritorial laws. The exception, moreover, is the basis in international law for the government's attempt to enforce the Soviet pipeline sanctions on foreign subsidiaries, attributing to them the nationality of their parent company.[44]

The real issue in this respect is the extent to which U.S. nationality can be attributed to subsidiaries such as

Dresser-France.  There is no well-established body of law
governing the nationality of subsidiaries or corporations
generally, and a company could be treated as a "citizen" of
five or six countries due to the confusing interrelation-
ships, or lack thereof, in national laws.  One common rule,
of course, is that a corporation will be deemed a citizen of
the state or country in which it is created.[45]  This begs
the question of whether the French subsidiary of a U.S. company can be deemed a U.S. citizen as well as a French citizen on the basis of its U.S. ownership.  During the pipeline
controversy in 1982, a Dutch court held that a U.S. subsidiary incorporated and having its principal place of business
in the Netherlands had to be treated as a Dutch corporation.[46]  At roughly the same time, the U.S. Supreme Court
held, in the Sumitomo case, that a wholly owned Japanese subsidiary incorporated in the state of New York had to be con-
strued as a U.S. corporation subject to U.S. laws.[47]

        The pipeline controls case is an ideal example of the
need to balance competing national policies.  To reconcile
such dilemmas, certain legal standards have been developed
for recognizing and balancing the competing interests of nations asserting jurisdictions.  These standards, which do
not have the full force of law but which have been recognized
by many U.S. courts,[48] essentially provide that when two
states seek to exercise concurrent jurisdiction in a matter
that requires inconsistent conduct, the states should consider moderating enforcement in light of:

1.  vital national interests of each of the states,
2.  the extent and nature of the hardship that inconsistent
    enforcement would impose on the person,
3.  the extent to which the required conduct is to take
    place in the territory of the other state,
4.  the nationality of the person concerned, and
5.  the extent to which the enforcement action of either
    state can reasonably be expected to achieve compliance.

        Obviously, an analysis of such factors cannot always
resolve contradictions such as those faced by Dresser-France
and other foreign companies in the pipeline case.  They are,
however, the closest thing to direct guidance on the international legal scenario for governments  seeking extraterri-

torial enforcements.  In the pipeline controversy, the stated foreign policy purpose of the U.S. controls had to be balanced against a host of European interests, including the need for diversification of energy sources, the promise of billions of dollars in increased trade, and the creation of thousands of new jobs in places of high unemployment.  As the parties most directly affected by such interests, international law would counsel that European countries be permitted to pursue their contractual plans.

A look at the possible hardship implicit in inconsistent enforcement leaves the unsettling impression, in the pipeline case, that severe penalties would be imposed on one side or another of the Atlantic no matter what course exporters chose.  If nothing else, this factor underscores the need for moderation on the part of all governments concerned. In looking at the prospect of compliance with the conflicting directives, it can be seen that France, Great Britain, and Italy all ordered their domestic corporations to fulfill their contracts with the Soviet Union in defiance of the U.S. controls, and all such companies agreed to pursue their contracts.

In applying such decisions and standards, it becomes difficult to make a legal case for the proposition that a European company that happens to be a subsidiary of a U.S. company should be deemed a U.S. national subject to the extensive U.S. controls over commercial affairs between that company and a third country.  Despite any U.S. intention of extraterritorial enforcement, the nationality principle of international law does not support that enforcement.


CONCLUSION


Despite these remarks, one must not pretend that the United States will be particularly constrained by the letter of international law in administering its export control framework.  Indeed, the Soviet pipeline case is a supreme example of how foreign policy concerns and diplomatic power will at times overshadow legal standards.  International law "bends to the will of Congress."[49]  But with such power to bend international legal principles also comes responsibility.  The political considerations that aroused the strong negative reaction from U.S. allies in the pipeline case, and the territorial principles behind that reaction, are best understood when one thinks of how the United States would have reacted if the situation had been reversed. One might consider the hypothetical case in which a Dutch company had a majority interest in a U.S. tractor manufacturer that had begun to produce tractors in a $100 million contract with a South American country. Can anyone doubt what the U.S. reaction would be if the Dutch government, concluding that the U.S. company was a "person subject to the jurisdiction" of Holland, specifically ordered that the U.S. company not comply with the $100 million contract?

It is unequivocally clear that the Soviet pipeline controls and most other embargoes extended to foreign entities have only the most tenuous support in the international legal framework. It may be somewhat extravagant to infer from the political actions taken after the imposition of the pipeline embargo that the controls were ultimately withdrawn because of the lack of support international law. Yet, it should be seen by now that the realities that forced that withdrawal are closely related to the policies behind the legal standards that prevail against such an embargo. When one assesses those policies, along with the severe diplomatic reactions, the loss of millions of dollars in export trade, the undermining of U.S. credibility as a dependable supplier of goods, and the general disruption in the international business community caused by the pipeline and other extraterritorial controls, one might make a convincing case against the inclusion of such extraterritorial jurisdiction in any new export control laws. Indeed, one might even begin to pause over the remarks of French President Mitterand, which were so casually dismissed when they were made, that an embargo is an act of economic warfare that should be invoked only by a nation that is prepared to proceed to military hostilities.

In closing, the problems of export controls bring to mind an analogy to the oft-quoted words used by Dr. Samuel Johnson to describe an activity more salubrious than that of embargoes. "The expense is damnable, the position ridiculous, and the pleasure fleeting." The pleasure from the pipeline embargo was felt only by a few closeted foreign-policy makers and was very temporary indeed. The position it put the United States in with its allies was so ridiculous as to be absurd. And the expense was overwhelming, making U.S. companies feel that they had been on the receiving end of the act to which Dr. Johnson alluded.


NOTES

1. The expanded controls announced on June 18, 1982, extended controls on exports of petroleum transmission and refinery equipment that had been issued on December 30, 1981. See, 15 C.F.R. §376, 379, 385, 399 (1982). Amendment of Oil and Gas Controls to U.S.S.R., 47 Federal Register 250 (1982), reprinted in 21 International Legal Materials 854 (1982); Statement on Extension of U.S. Sanctions, 18 Weekly Compilation of Presidential Documents 820 (June 21, 1982).

2. See New York Times, July 23, 1982, p. 1, column 6.

3. See New York Times, July 24, 1982, p. 5, column 2.

4. European Communities Comments on the U.S. Regulations Concerning Trade with the U.S.S.R., 21 International Legal Materials 891 (1982).

5. British Statement and Order Invoking Protection of Trading Interests Act, 21 International Legal Materials 851 (1982).

6. The protest of U.S. allies over the interference of U.S. export controls in the sovereign powers is further discussed at Use of Export Controls and Export Credits for Foreign Policy Purposes, Hearing before the Committee on Banking, Housing and Urban Affairs, 95th Cong., 2d Sess., 10 (1978); Extension and Revision of the Export Administration Act, Hearings before the Committee on Foreign Affairs, 96th Cong., 1st Sess., 489; Corcoran, The Trading with the Enemy Act and the Controlled Canadian Corporation (1968) McGill L.J. 174.

7. See, for example, Baum "The Global Corporation: An American Challenge to the Nation-State?" 55 Iowa Law Review 410 (1969); 39 Department of State Bulletin 209 (1958).

8. See Wall Street Journal, March 7, 1974, p. 18, column 3.

9. See New York Times, April 19, 1974, p. 1, column 6.

10. See A. Lowenfeld, Trade Controls for Political Ends, 81 (1977); Note "Extraterritorial Application of the Export Administration Amendments of 1977," 8 Georgia Journal of International and Comparative Law 741, 749 (1978).

11. Under the French concept of <u>abus de droit</u>, French courts have the right to overrule corporate management's decisions should it be deemed that the decisions are contrary to the interest of the corporation.

12. See Craig, "Application of the Trading of the Enemy Act to Foreign Corporations Owned by Americans: Reflections on <u>Fruehauf v. Massardi</u>," 83 <u>Harvard Law Review</u> 579 (1970).

13. In "Raytheon Manufacturing Co.," 24 <u>Federal Register</u> 2626 (1959), Raytheon exported controlled microwave equipment to an English customer that then integrated the Raytheon equipment into a larger product and transshipped it to an unauthorized third country. The U.S. government applied sanctions to Raytheon and its English customer.

14. See Abbott, "Linking Trade and Political Goals: Foreign Policy Export Controls in the 1970's and 1980's," 65 <u>Minnesota Law Review</u> 739, 782, 840-49 (1981).

15. 50 U.S.C. §1701-1706.

16. Revision of Export Controls Affecting the USSR and Poland, 47 <u>Federal Register</u> 51,858-60 (1982).

17. The foreign concerns seriously affected by the pipeline controls were Dresser France S.A. 47 <u>Federal Register</u> 39,708-10 (1982), reprinted in 21 <u>International Legal Materials</u> 1099-100 (1982); Nuovo Pignone S.P.A. Industrie Meccaniche E. Founderia, 47 <u>Federal Register</u> 39,708-10 (1982); John Brown Engineering Ltd., 47 <u>Federal Register</u> 40,205-06 (1982), reprinted in 21 <u>International Legal Materials</u> 1101-02 (1982); Cruesot-Loire S.A. 47 <u>Federal Register</u> 42,392 (1982), reprinted in 21 <u>International Legal Materials</u> 1102-03 (1982); AEG-Kanis Turbinenfabrik GmbH, 47 <u>Federal Register</u> 44,603-05 (1982), reprinted in 21 <u>International Legal Materials</u> 1103-04 (1982) and Mannesmann Anlagenbau Aktiengesellschaft, 47 <u>Federal Register</u> 44,603-05 (1982).

18. On December 31, 1981, the U.S. government had announced the first series of pipeline restrictions, "Exports and Re-exports to the Soviet Union of Oil and Gas Equipment, Goods and Technology Originating in the United States," 27 <u>Federal Register</u> 141 (1982), 47 <u>Federal Register</u> 144 (1982).

19. <u>Dresser Industries v. Baldridge</u>, No. 82-2385 (D.D.C. filed August 23, 1982).

20. Dresser-France S.A., "Order Temporarily Denying Export Privileges," 47 <u>Federal Register</u> 38,170 (1982).

21. Dresser-France S.A., "Order Modifying Temporary Denial of Export Privileges," 47 Federal Register 39,708-10 (1982).

22. Matter of District of Columbia Workmen's Compensation Act, 554 F.2d 1075-1079 (D.C. Circuit 1976); South East Chicago Commission v. Department of Housing and Urban Development, 488 F.2d 1119-1123 (7th Circuit 1973); de Rodulfa v. United States, 461 F.2d 1240-1247 (D.C. Circuit 192), cert. denied, 409 U.S. 949 (1972).

23. See 50 U.S.C. App. 2401-2420.

24. 50 U.S.C. App. §2405(b)(4).

25. Restatement (Second) of Foreign Relations Law Section 38; See also Foley Brothers v. Filardo, 336 U.S. 281, 285 (1949).

26. Attorneys representing Dresser-France in its Soviet pipeline controls suit against the U.S. government asserted as a primary argument that Congress had not sufficiently expressed its consent to authorize export controls that would violate international law. See Memorandum of Points and Authorities in Support of Motion for Temporary Restraining Order 15, Dresser Industries v. Baldrige (D.D.C. Aug. 24, 1982).

27. Vermila-Brown Company v. Connell, 335 U.S. 377 (1948); Blackmer v. United States, 284 U.S. 421 (1932).

28. Stegman v. United States, 425 F.2d 984 (9th Cir.) cert. denied, 400 U.S. 837 (1970).

29. See, for example, Abbott (1981) p. 846.

30. H.R. Rep. No. 459, 95th Cong., 1st Sess., 21 (1977). The present authority to extend U.S. controls to foreign parties subject to U.S. jurisdiction was added to the Export Administration Act in 1977 in legislation that amended the Trading with the Enemy Act and promulgated the International Emergency Powers Act. In these measures Congress granted the same jurisdictional reach in U.S. controls as those provided under the Trading with the Enemy Act. S. Rep. No. 466, 95th Cong., 1st Sess., 6 (1977); Revision of the Trading with the Enemy Act, Committee on International Relations, 95th Cong., 1st Sess., 7 (1977).

31. S. Rep. No. 466, 95th Cong., 1st Sess., 6 (1977).

32. The Export Administration Act also, of course, applies extraterritorially to technical data and merchandise originating in the United States. This authority, on which

U.S. export controls on the reexport of goods from foreign countries are based, was clearly expressed by the 95th Congress. See, for example, H. Rep. No. 459, 95th Cong., 1st Sess., 17 (1977).

33. This firmly entrenched rule has been reflected in a number of judicial decisions. See, for example, McCullock v. Sociedad Nacionale De Marineros de Honduras, 372 U.S. 10 (1963); Benz v. Compania Naviera Hidalgo, 353 U.S. 138, 147 (1957).

34. See Stern, "Specters and Pipedreams," 48 Foreign Policy 21, 35 (1982), in which, for example, it was noted that the "extension of the pipeline sanctions has created a major rift in the [Western] alliance."

35. In the United States, international law is an inherent part of the legal system, to be reassigned and applied by the courts. See L. Henken, Foreign Affairs and the Constitution, 221 (1972). In England, international law is without effect unless it is set in such cases as it may be specifically incorporated into the laws of the country through Parliamentary Act. See I. Brownlie, Principles of Public International Law, 45–53 (3rd ed. 1979).

36. See, for example, Juan L. Oppenheim, International Law, 286 (8th ed. 1955).

37. Id.

38. Id. at 325; 5 N. Whiteman, Digest of International Law, 183–86 (1965).

39. In the words of the U.S. Supreme Court, the "jurisdiction of the nation within its own territory is necessarily exclusive and absolute," Schooner Exchange v. McFaddon, 11 U.S. (7 Cranch) 116, 136, 1812.

40. See Lowe, "Blocking Extraterritorial Jurisdiction: The British Protection of Trading Interests Act," 1980, and 75 American Journal of International Law 1981; Note, "Enjoining the Application of the British National Trading Act and Private American Antitrust Litigation," 79 Michigan Law Review 1574 (1981).

41. See, for example, New York Times, September 11, 1982, p. 19, column 2.

42. Juan L. Oppenheim, International Law, p. 288; 5 Whiteman, p. 187.

43. See, for example, F. Mann, Studies in International Law, 110–39 (1973), in which it is stated that the

first and foremost restriction imposed on a state is that it may not exercise its power in any form in the territory of another state.

44. See 5 N. Whiteman, pp. 6-7; Revard v. U.S., 375 F.2d 882 (5th Circuit) cert. denied, sub. nom. Growlow v. U.S., 389 U.S. 884 (1957).

45. Most commercial treaties entered into by the United States provide that a company's nationality is determined by its place of incorporation. W. Friedman, O. Lissitzin, and R. Pugh, Cases on Materials of International Law, 513 (1969).

46. Compagnie Europeane des Petroles S.A. v. Sensor Nederland B.V., No. 82/716 (District Court) The Hague, September 17, 1982. In this case involving the extension of U.S. export controls to export from a Dutch affiliate of a U.S. firm, a Dutch court held that the subject controls violated international law.

47. Sumitomo Shoji America, Inc. v. Avaglanio, 102 Superior Court, 2374 (1982).

48. Statement (Second) of Foreign Relations Law, Section 40; see U.S. Bank of Nova Scotia, 691 F.2d 1384, 1389 (11th Circuit 1982); U.S. v. Vepco, Inc., 644 F.2d, 1324, 1331 (9th Circuit 1981).

49. The Over the Top, 5 F.2d 838, 842 (D. Conn. 1925); Zenith Radio Corp. v. Matsushita Electric Industries Co., F. Supp. 1161, 1179 (Eastern District of Pennsylvania 1980).

# 11

# FIATALLIS NORTH AMERICA, INC., AND THE PIPELINE SANCTIONS

## David H. Buswell

Fiatallis North America is one of three operating units of Fiatallis, a worldwide manufacturer of construction machinery headquartered in Turin, Italy, and part of the Fiat Group of companies. Fiatallis North America is an American corporation headquartered in Deerfield, Illinois, with a manufacturing plant in Springfield, Illinois, parts depots in Carol Stream, Illinois; Dallas, Texas; Atlanta, Georgia; Cranberry, New Jersey; Hayward, California; and Ontario, Canada. Sales offices and dealers are in a number of other states and countries.

This chapter discusses the effects on Fiatallis North America, its employees, and its suppliers of the recent restrictions placed on exports of technology and equipment to the Soviet Union. First, however, it should be made clear that Fiatallis North America does not negotiate commercial transactions directly with buyers in the Soviet Union. Those negotiations are handled by Fiatallis Europe, which coordinates the capabilities and talents of a number of worldwide Fiat subsidiaries and related companies. And, while this chapter will be limited to Fiatallis North America, one surely can realize the difficulties that U.S. export limitations have caused the parent company, Fiat, which has invested millions of dollars to establish a U.S. manufacturing capability to support worldwide sales.

On December 29, 1981, President Reagan issued a statement concerning recent events in Poland, placing a "heavy and direct responsibility" on the Soviet Union for those events and announcing a series of retaliatory measures including:

> The issuance of renewal of licenses for the export to the USSR of electronic equipment, computers and other high-technology materials is being suspended.

> Licenses will be required for export to the Soviet Union for an expanded list of oil and gas equipment. Issuance of such licenses will be suspended. This includes pipelayers.

On the same date, the Department of Commerce announced that, at the direction of the President, it would "stop processing license applications on oil and gas equipment and on high technology items to the Soviet Union."[1] Two days later, the Commerce Department announced that it was issuing new regulations, effective December 30, 1981, that would "suspend processing of all applications for validated licenses to export to the USSR." The department stated that the new controls "were imposed at the direction of President Reagan as a result of the role played by the Soviets in repressing Poland."[2] Consistent with this announcement, a General Order effective December 30, 1981, appeared in the Federal Register on January 5, 1982, "suspending the processing of all licensing for exports to the USSR to further U.S. foreign policy objectives in light of the Soviet Union's heavy and direct responsibility for the repression in Poland."[3] Just prior to the imposition of the sanctions, Fiatallis North America had in progress two transactions for sales to the Soviet Union: one for the transfer of design data for its model 41B crawler tractor (for which an application for validated license had been filed on November 4, 1981); and a second for the sale of between 100 and 200 model FP120 sideboom tractors, commonly used in pipe laying and referred to as pipelayers. Both transactions were suspended as of January 5, 1982.

The Soviet Union wanted the design data for the crawler tractors because it wished to produce a tractor of this size at an existing plant in Cheboksary. The model 41B was initially designed in 1965 and was updated in the 1970s. It is a large, heavy, slow tractor used for dozing and ripping earth and rock and for push-loading motor scrapers in surface mines, road construction, dam building, and other large earth-moving projects. The tractor has no military use (although Fiatallis had to spend a great deal of time and effort convincing the Department of Defense that its 41B could not be converted into a tank) and cannot be used in oil exploration, extraction, transportation, or refining. Few of these machines have been manufactured in recent years because of their limited uses and difficulty in movement. An application for an export license was required only because technology transfers of all kinds to the Soviet Union, even of the least sensitive character, require licenses.

In addition to the drawings for the model 41B, for which Fiatallis would have received some $110 million, the Soviets wished to purchase unassembled "kits" of the bulldozer in order to develop their manufacturing skills. These kit sales were to have continued for at least four years, providing another $360 million to Fiatallis. (It is interesting to note that, even during the sanctions, these "kits" and even the assembled machines could be sold and delivered under general license. The problem, of course, was that the drawings had to be provided before the remainder of the deal could be effective.) In addition, Fiatallis was led to believe that should the technology transfer take place, the Soviet Union would give Fiatallis 60 percent of its annual requirement for 300 horsepower and above bulldozers for four years. This would have meant another $960 million to Fiatallis.

The Department of Commerce returned the license application to Fiatallis North America without comment as a result of the department's General Order suspending the processing of all licensing for exports to the Soviet Union. Fiatallis executives believed then and now that the order was inconsistent with the President's statement and unnecessarily disruptive in that it pertained to all licensing, while the President's statement only referred to licensing of high-technology materials.

In late 1981, concomitant with the negotiations involving the drawings for the 41B bulldozer, the Soviets had expressed considerable interest in the Fiatallis model FP120 pipelayers. Specifically, they had tested a prototype machine that had been, to a great degree, designed to their specifications, and they indicated a willingness to make an initial purchase of between 100 and 200 machines. Fiatallis calculated that, over a four- or five-year period, pipelayer sales to the Soviets would be worth approximately $280 million, plus an additional $50 million for spare parts for these machines and other models involved in the technology transfer.

In accordance with the President's announcement, the Commerce Department's General Order, effective December 30, 1981, expanded the list of petroleum-related equipment requiring validated licenses to include not only equipment related to the exploration and development of petroleum reserves but also equipment related to the transmission and refining of petroleum; this included pipelayers.

Clearly, the President included pipelayers in his statement as a means of delaying the Yamal pipeline. Interestingly, the Department of Commerce had previously referred to pipelayers as "low technology equipment . . . not designated as strategic and . . . not multilaterally controlled by our allies. . . ." The department also noted that "similar equipment is readily available from other foreign suppliers."[4]

Needless to say, Fiatallis was very concerned with the effect the sanctions would have on its business. As the statistics in Table 11.1 indicate, the company had already experienced a drastic decline in domestic sales of earth-moving equipment.[5]

This large negative year-to-year comparison illustrates the importance to the U.S. construction machinery industry of all incremental business. Daily newspapers and business magazines alike contained repeated warnings to investors about the depressed state of various construction machinery manufacturers. Fiatallis North America had suffered along with the industry and had been forced to make dramatic cutbacks in staff, labor force, and facilities in

TABLE 11.1

Industry-Wide Statistics
(by units; Fiatallis size classes; in percentages)

North American Shipments (Wholesale)

| | 1979 vs. 1978 | 1980 vs. 1979 | 1981 vs. 1980 | 1st Quarter 1982 vs. 1981 |
|---|---|---|---|---|
| Crawler tractors | -16 | -18 | -9 | -52 |
| Crawler loaders | -21 | -40 | -23 | -64 |
| Wheel loaders | +3 | -27 | -9 | -43 |

North American Deliveries (Retail)

| | 1979 vs. 1978* | 1980 vs. 1979 | 1981 vs. 1980 | 1st Quarter 1982 vs. 1981 |
|---|---|---|---|---|
| Crawler tractors | -17 | -19 | -12 | -36 |
| Crawler loaders | -20 | -39 | -16 | -46 |
| Wheel loaders | +2 | -23 | -12 | -26 |

*Estimated.

Deerfield and Springfield, Illinois, and in its parts
depots and field personnel throughout the United States.
Table 11.2 illustrates these force reductions:[6]

TABLE 11.2

Fiatallis North America, Inc. Employment Levels
(yearly average)

| | 1978 | 1979 | 1980 | 1981 | 1982 (1st quarter) |
|---|---|---|---|---|---|
| Employees | 4,400 | 3,800 | 3,000 | 2,300 | 2,100 |

Beginning in mid-January 1982, Fiatallis and others
affected by the sanctions attempted to tell their story to
virtually anyone in the legislative and executive branches
who would listen. By mid-February, Fiatallis executives
had told their story to at least 50 high-ranking individuals
in Congress and the Reagan administration. Other companies—
including Caterpillar, Deere and Co., Dresser Industries,
Sundstrand, Cooper Industries, Dayco Corp., General Electric—also were explaining the futility of the embargo.

Virtually every major business and trade organization
was vehemently opposed to the sanctions and worked in
tandem with individual companies to seek their repeal.
These efforts continued into the spring of 1982 and, by
the time of the Versailles Summit meeting, nearly everyone
involved believed that the President would either repeal or
substantially relax the sanctions. Imagine the reaction,
then, when within days after the conclusion of the summit,
President Reagan announced, through the Commerce Department,
regulations amending the export controls to extend U.S. law
overseas to licensees and subsidiaries of U.S. corporations.
The Reagan administration, instead of softening its position, clearly was bent on taking an even harder line.

Fiatallis and a number of other companies then met with Congressman Paul Findley of Illinois. The Ad Hoc Committee to Lift the Sanctions was formed and immediately backed Congressman Findley's bill designed to do just that. (Ironically, Congressman Findley was defeated in 1982 primarily because of high unemployment in Springfield, Illinois, the site of Fiatallis's North American manufacturing facility.) H.R. 6838 would have amended Section 6 of the Export Administration Act of 1979 by adding the following language:

> Termination of certain controls: those export controls imposed under this section on December 30, 1981 and June 22, 1982 on goods or technology shall not be effective on or after the date of the enactment of this subsection.

On August 5, 1982, the House Foreign Affairs subcommittee on International Economic Policy and Trade approved the bill by a five to two vote. On August 10, the full committee voted, 22 to 12, to send the bill to the floor. The legislation ultimately was defeated in early October, but the message was clear. On November 13, 1982, the sanctions were effectively lifted.

But for Fiatallis, the damage had been done. First, the company had lost nearly $2 billion of potential business. During the duration of the sanctions, its Japanese competitor, Komatsu, had sold over 900 machines to the Soviets at an average price of $400,000 per machine.

Since the lifting of the embargo, Fiatallis's Soviet sales have been virtually nonexistent not only in pipelayers but also in the larger bulldozers that the Soviets traditionally had purchased from Fiatallis each year for mining operations. The Soviets apparently are giving U.S. suppliers a taste of what it is like to be "cut off." To date, Komatsu has increased the number of units sold to the Soviet Union from 900 to over 2,000.

What are the lessons to be learned from the sanctions? Basically, the negative results reaffirmed the criteria outlined by Congress in 1979 when it reauthorized the Export Administration Act. Specifically, Congress said that the criteria to be considered before export controls are put into effect are:

1.  The controls should have a good chance of working.
2.  There should be consistency between control policies and other U.S. foreign policies toward the target nation.
3.  The reaction of other nations should be considered before imposing controls.
4.  The impact of controls on U.S. competitiveness must be evaluated.
5.  The controls should be able to be enforced.
6.  The consequences of not imposing controls should be considered.

The sanctions not only failed to achieve their intended efect but also seriously strained NATO and severely damaged U.S. business by calling into question our reliability as a trading partner and by handing millions of dollars of business to the Japanese.

NOTES

1.  Department of Commerce, International Trade Administration, "Press Release," 81-227, December 29, 1981.
2.  Department of Commerce, International Trade Administration, "Press Release," 81-230, December 31, 1981.
3.  Federal Register, vol. 47, no. 141.
4.  Department of Commerce, International Trade Administration, "Press Release," 81-136, July 31, 1981.
5.  Data are from various internal company documents.
6.  Ibid.

# 12

# THE CASE OF JOHN BROWN ENGINEERING AND THE SOVIET GAS PIPELINE

## Stanley D. Nollen

THE PROBLEM

On November 13, 1982, the U.S. government lifted its embargoes and sanctions against the U.S., British, and European companies that had business with the Soviet natural gas pipelines. This action relieved, at least for the moment, a firestorm of controversy that had been building for nearly a year. Business returned, but not to normal. U.S.-European harmony officially resumed, but the issues only began to be joined.

It started in 1980 when several European nations agreed, despite U.S. opposition, to buy large quantities of natural gas from Siberian fields. British and European companies, as well as U.S. firms, successfully competed for Soviet business to build the pipeline to transport the gas from Siberia to Western Europe. The trade deal, worth roughly $11 to $15 billion as announced by the financial press in September 1981, was the biggest East-West deal ever. But the imposition of martial law in Poland in December 1981 led President Reagan to place an embargo, which affected U.S. and foreign countries alike, on the export of oil and gas equipment and technology. The administration extended the embargo in June 1982 to cover foreign subsidiaries and licensees of U.S. comanies, exacerbating protests by British and European governments that the embargo was an illegal, extraterritorial application of U.S. law to foreign companies. When the companies

defied the embargo, the United States imposed sanctions.  Intense diplomatic activity yielded a resolution in November
1982, but the underlying issues remain and a repetition of
these problems could easily occur.

The 1982 Soviet gas pipeline controversy was perhaps
the most ruinous case of its kind in NATO's history, but it
was not the first such case.  Exactly 20 years earlier, the
United States had used an embargo to try to block the construction of a Soviet oil pipeline to Eastern Europe.  On
that occasion, Britain ignored the embargo and supplied steel
pipe to the USSR, although some German firms broke their
contracts.[1]  Differences between Washington and London (as
well as differences between Washington and various European
capitals) over foreign trade go back over 30 years.  Perhaps
this most recent, biggest, and worst dispute contains the
lessons that will prevent further controversies.

Throughout the 1982 Soviet pipeline case, business
firms were at the center of the controversy.  The dispute
between the United States and European governments caught
companies such as John Brown in the middle.  The case is one
of business-government relations on an international scale.
It is also a case of private business strategy in crisis.

Like any retrospective investigation, the purpose of
this chapter is to extract lessons for the future--lessons
for business policy and for public policy.  The perspective
in this study is that of the firm, and in particular the
principal British firm in the case, John Brown Engineering
Limited.


WHO IS JOHN BROWN ENGINEERING?

As will soon become clear, the nature of John Brown's
business determined (more than merely influenced) much of
its experience in the pipeline sanction controversy.  John
Brown Engineering Limited (JBE) is one of several major companies that make up the John Brown Group of Companies (officially John Brown PLC, or public limited company).

JBE has one product, an industrial gas turbine, which
it makes in five different sizes, all at its single location
in Clydebank, Scotland, near Glasgow.  The gas turbine is
used either for power generation or in mechanical drive ap-

plication such as pumping fluids. Since it began building
such turbines in 1965, JBE has delivered a total of 385 of
them to its customers. In the past five years, it has
shipped from 18 to 41 turbines annually.[2]

In the mid-1960s, JBE, which had been a shipbuilder
and supplier of engineered marine equipment since 1899, was
beginning to make and sell small gas turbines. Then it took
the step that would fundamentally change the company's direction and lead to its entanglement in the 1982 Soviet pipeline
controversy. That step was to become a manufacturing associate of General Electric (GE) of the United States.

The thrust of the GE-JBE agreement is that GE supplies
technology and some parts (the rotor) while JBE manufactures
and sells the turbine. What GE gets out of this agreement
is sales of its rotor and its technology. What JBE gets is
participation in the worldwide large gas turbine market. JBE
is not restricted in its marketing domain (although its only
sales in the contiguous United States are to GE itself) and
is not a licensee of GE, a distinction of some subsequent importance for the Soviet pipeline case.

JBE's business is mostly export business--92 percent
of its turbines are sold to foreign customers in 45 countries around the world, with the Middle East accounting for
the largest share of JBE business (see Table 12.1). The company is no stranger to political risk, having done business
in Iraq, Syria, Libya, Algeria, and Argentina, as well as in
the Soviet Union itself.

Indeed, the Soviet Union has been one of the largest
single purchasers of gas turbines in the world in the last
several years and has also been JBE's best customer. Since
JBE's first sale to the Soviet Union in 1975, the company
has sold 67 turbines for Soviet natural gas transmission
pipelines (up to January 1983), accounting for about 30 percent of its business. Even before the recent large and controversial order, Soviet business amounted to 25 percent of
all JBE gas turbine orders (from 1975 to 1981).[3]

Like JBE, John Brown PLC is internationally oriented.
In 1982, 60 percent of the parent firm's sales were outside
the United Kingdom, 24 percent of all sales were exports by
its British companies, and 36 percent were sales by its foreign subsidiaries. The Americas are John Brown's biggest international market, mostly through the sales of its 12 U.S.

TABLE 12.1

John Brown Engineering Gas Turbine Sales by Region, 1967–83

| Region | Number of Turbines |
|---|---|
| Middle East | 110 |
| Western Hemisphere | 68 |
| USSR | 67 |
| Far East | 61 |
| Africa | 41 |
| UK and North Sea | 31 |
| Europe | 7 |
| Total | 365 |

Source: John Brown Engineering official publications.

TABLE 12.2

John Brown PLC International Business, 1982

| Region | International Sales[a] (£ million) | Percent of International Sales from Foreign Subsidiaries |
|---|---|---|
| Americas | 187 | 94 |
| Asia | 113 | 3 |
| Europe (includes USSR) | 56 | 42 |
| Africa | 31 | 86 |
| Australasia | 20 | 93 |
| Total international | 407 | 61 |
| United Kingdom | 274 | n.a. |
| Total worldwide | 681 | 36 |

[a]Exports from UK companies plus sales of foreign subsidiaries.

Source: John Brown PLC Annual Report 1982.

companies and one Canadian company (see Table 12.2). The
U.S. companies construct oil and petrochemical plants, make
machinery for the plastics and textile industries, and manufacture machine tools (see Table 12.3).

The Soviet Union is also important to the John Brown
Group. "The USSR has represented a significant market not
just for John Brown Engineering but for other companies in
the John Brown Group over the past 25 years."[4]  Soviet business for John Brown dates from the 1860s, when Mr. John
Brown first sold steel for railways to Russia.

This information about John Brown is important for
those trying to understand the Soviet gas pipeline controversy. Consider the following key facts:

1.  The gas turbine is John Brown Engineering's one and only
    product. At an average price of £3 million each, every
    sale is crucial.
2.  Soviet business is critical to the success of JBE and
    very important to the John Brown Group. Trade with the
    Soviet Union is a usual and long-standing feature of
    John Brown business.
3.  John Brown companies are closely linked to the United
    States. John Brown Engineering is dependent on General
    Electric, a U.S. company, for its product, at least in
    the short run. The John Brown Group as a whole has in-
    vested heavily in the United States.
4.  John Brown Engineering is important to the British gov-
    ernment. It contributes to a favorable trade balance and
    is located near Glasgow in an area of high unemployment.

It would appear from these conditions of John Brown's
business that a dispute between the United States, Great
Britain, and the Soviet Union could not be worse for the
company. But of course that is exactly what happened.


CHRONOLOGY OF EVENTS

Before one can begin to discuss the effects of the
yearlong pipeline controversy, one needs to understand the
facts behind the case. On October 6, 1981, JBE announced
that it had signed a contract for £61 million to supply 21

TABLE 12.3

John Brown PLC Companies and Businesses and 1982 Sales and Profits (Losses)

| Business | Sales[a] (£ million) | Profits[b] (£ million) | Major Companies |
|---|---|---|---|
| Engineering and construction | 326.0 | 14.4 | John Brown Engineering & Construction<br>Crawford & Russell |
| Industrial products | | | |
| Plastics and textile machinery | 119.6 | 4.2 | Leesona |
| Machine tools | 77.2 | (2.4) | Wickman<br>Olofsson |
| Gas turbines | 93.8 | 1.8 | John Brown Engineering |
| General engineering and miscellaneous<br>Commercial vehicle bodies,<br>agricultural equipment<br>Heavy engineering<br>Stainless and specialty steels | 64.2 | (.1) | Craven Tasker<br>Markham<br>Firth Brown |
| Total group | 680.8 | 14.2[c] | |

[a]Fiscal year ended March 31, 1982.
[b]Before taxes.
[c]After deduction of corporate charges less income.
Source: John Brown PLC Annual Report 1982.

116

gas turbines for the Soviet natural gas pipeline to Western Europe. JBE was one of six European companies to win major contracts for the pipeline from V/O Machinoimport, the Soviet foreign trade organization (see Table 12.4). Delivery was to commence in the late summer of 1982.[5] Subsequently, JBE announced (on October 13) that it had obtained further orders for spare parts and service for the pipeline worth £43 million. The total contract value to JBE was $195 million, the largest contract in the company's history. By itself, the contract accounted for about two-thirds of the company's entire order book.[6]

TABLE 12.4

Major European Contractors for the Soviet Gas Pipeline

| | |
|---|---|
| General and management contractors for 41 compressor stations | |
| Mannesman (Germany) with Creusot Loire (France) | 22 stations |
| Nuovo Pignone (Italy) | 19 stations |
| | |
| Gas turbine contractors | |
| Nuovo Pignone (Italy) | 57 turbines |
| AEG-Kanis (Germany) | 47 turbines |
| John Brown Engineering (Britain)[a] | 21 turbines |
| Alsthom Atlantique (France)[b] | 40 turbine rotors |

[a]John Brown's contract is with Mannesman and Creusot-Loire.

[b]Spares to be supplied later.

Source: Economist.

On December 29, 1981, President Reagan, using the authority granted him in the Export Administration Act, placed an embargo on the export of all U.S.-origin oil and gas transmission and refinement equipment, services, and tech-

nology to the Soviet Union. (Exploration and production
equipment and technology of U.S. origin had already been
under embargo since the 1979 Soviet invasion of Afghanistan.)
The embargo included the transmission of data and also applied to the reexport of U.S. goods from foreign locations.

> Effective December 30, 1981, the processing of
> all applications for validated licenses, re-
> export authorizations for shipment of any com-
> modities or transfer of any technical data to
> the USSR has been suspended. Furthermore, out-
> standing validated licenses and authorizations
> to export may be reviewed to determine whether
> suspension or revocation is necessary.[7]

The objective of the embargo, which followed closely the imposition of martial law in Poland, was "to further U.S. foreign policy objectives in light of the Soviet Union's heavy
and direct responsibility for the repression in Poland."[8]
    JBE had been exporting under a previously obtained
general license. Following the President's announcement, a
validated license would be required but would not be acted
on. The embargo thus prevented General Electric from shipping any rotors to JBE for use in turbines destined for the
Soviet pipeline and from communicating data about the turbines. The embargo also prevented JBE from shipping any
turbines that contained General Electric parts. Both AEG-
Kanis and Nuovo Pinone (the other turbine makers) were simi-
larly affected because they had the same relationship with
General Electric that JBE did. The status of Alsthom Atlantique was not immediately clear.
    On June 18, 1982, President Reagan extended the embargo
to subsidiaries of U.S. companies operating outside the United
States and to licensees of U.S. technology.

> At the direction of the President, export con-
> trols on oil and gas goods and technology to the
> USSR are amended to include exports of non-U.S.-
> origin goods and technical data by U.S. owned or
> controlled companies wherever organized or doing
> business as well as certain foreign-produced
> products of U.S. technical data not previously
> subject to controls.[9]

This extension had no further effect on JBE because it was neither a subsidiary nor a licensee of a U.S. company (it was and is a manufacturing associate) and because JBE's business (and that of the other turbine makers) with the Soviet pipeline was already completely embargoed. The new extraterritorial provisions of the embargo, however, meant that other companies registered in Britain and Europe that had pipeline contracts were prevented from fulfilling those contracts.

On August 2, 1982, the British government, angered by the new U.S. action, directed British companies not to comply with the U.S. embargo affecting their business with the Soviet pipeline. The directive, issued by the Department of Trade, was based on the U.K. Protection of Trading Interests Act of 1980.[10] (Earlier, on June 30, the U.S. embargoes had been found by the Secretary of State for Trade to be damaging to the trading interests of the country.) The British companies so directed were JBE, Smith International, Baker Oil Tools, and American Air Filters. The latter three companies were all U.S. company subsidiaries, and American Air Filters was a JBE subcontractor (see Table 12.5).

On the same day, JBE announced that it would comply with the British directive and begin deliveries on its contract with Mannesman Creusot-Loire in association with V/O Machinoimport at the end of August, as specified in the contract.[11]

On September 9, 1982, JBE shipped six gas turbines from its Clydebank plant to the Soviet Union for use on the gas pipeline. On the same day, the U.S. government issued a temporary denial order that prohibited export of all U.S.-origin oil and gas equipment, services, and related technology to JBE from any company anywhere in the world. An identical denial order was issued on September 4 against Nuovo Pignone after that company shipped two turbines to the Soviet Union. This sanction would, if made permanent, have prevented JBE from making any turbines using GE rotors for any oil and gas industry customers. It was implemented by revoking the export licenses necessary for JBE to receive U.S.-origin equipment.

The next day, the British government directed two more British firms, Walter Kidde and Andrew Corporation, not to comply with the U.S. embargo.[12]

TABLE 12.5

British Firms with Major Soviet Gas Pipeline Business

| Company | Business | Contract Value (£ million) |
|---|---|---|
| John Brown Engineering[a] Clydebank, Scotland | Gas turbines (61) Spare parts, service (43a) | 104 |
| Ruston Gas Turbines (part of GEC) | Gas turbine generating sets | 29.7 |
| Plenty (part of Booker McConnell), Newbury | Fuel gas conditioning | 20 |
| Baker Oil Tools (U.K.)[a,b] Aberdeen, Scotland | Down-hole equipment | 14 |
| Smith International (North Sea)[a,b] Stroud, Gloucestershire | Well head equipment | 12.4 |
| Walter Kidde[a,b] Northolt, Middlesex | Fire protec- tion equipment | 9.5 |
| Rediffusion Sussex | Computer control equipment | 7.8 |
| American Air Filters[a,b,c] Cramlington, North- umberland | Air filters | 3.6 |
| Andrew Antennas[a,b] Lochgelly, Scotland | Radio antennas | 1 |
| Paladon Engineering | | 0.5 |

Note: A small number of other British firms have business with the Soviet gas pipeline; the total value of all British business with the pipeline exceeds £200 million.

[a]Directed by U.K. government not to comply with U.S. embargo.

[b]Subsidiary of U.S. company.

[c]Subcontractor to John Brown Engineering.

Sources: Financial Times, August 3, 1982, September 11, 1983; Economist, July 10, 1982; U.K. Department of Trade.

The United States lifted the sanctions and embargoes on November 13, 1982, and there was an informal intergovernmental understanding to consult about future East-West trade, including the issues of high-technology trade, energy dependence, and financing practices.  JBE progress toward fulfilling its contract for the Soviet pipeline was no longer impeded.

The chronology of events is a story of continuing escalation between governments, with JBE pulled three ways at once and put in an apparently impossible situation.  What did JBE do?  What could JBE have done?  How was JBE affected--economically and managerially--by this ever-worsening crisis?


ANALYZING JOHN BROWN'S RESPONSE

At the time of the controversy, JBE was an exclusively British company with a large Soviet contract, but it was dependent on American technology embodied in turbine rotors. Three months into the contract, the United States forbade the company to export its product.  It was then ordered by the British government not to comply with the U.S. prohibition, after which the United States applied sanctions to the company.  What options did JBE have in this case?  What position did it take, and what decisions did it make?


Options Before the Business Deal

The first question that arises is whether the entire unhappy episode could have been prevented by JBE in the first place.  Given the political climate, could JBE have foreseen trouble ahead?  Should the British government have forewarned JBE?  Had there been more doubt, would that have meant no Soviet pipeline contract?  The answers all around appear to be no.

JBE was an old hand at dealing with political risk and operating in countries with unstable governments, and the Soviet Union was a good long-term customer.  While the Soviets were hard-nosed negotiators, once they agreed to a contract, they always followed it strictly and paid on time. In addition, JBE had the expertise required to do business with the Soviets: adaptation to bureaucratic methods, submission of several modified sales quotations, meticulous preparation and fulfillment of contracts, long negotiations, and arrangement of credit facilities.[13]

But in this case the problem for JBE was the United States, not the Soviet Union. Because of the controversy over the building of the pipeline in the first place, it is clear that the JBE turbine contract could have been politically sensitive. The question was whether the existing general export license would apply to these turbines. Inquiries to the U.S. government before the Soviet contract was signed suggested that the answer was yes. (A newly validated export license might have been required; previously there had been an embargo on some oil and gas industry exploration and production equipment following the Afghanistan invasion.) Furthermore, the British government had discussed the Soviet pipeline business with JBE before the contract was agreed on in order to work out the commercial details of the export credits to be provided and there had been no signs of trouble.

Even had there been signs of trouble, there must have been powerful business incentives to accept some risk and go for the contract. Coming off a loss the year before, JBE needed new business badly. The order book was thin and the Soviet contract, the biggest ever for JBE, would triple it. And so the deal was made.


Options After the U.S. Embargoes

The United States imposed its first export embargo on December 29, 1981, and its second on June 18, 1982. The first one did the damage, at least as far as JBE was concerned. The second one infuriated the British government and worried the holding company, John Brown PLC.

The first U.S. embargo denied JBE the rotors it needed to make gas turbines because no export license could be obtained to allow them to be shipped to JBE. There were already six rotors (out of the 21 required) in stock at Clydebank, and so six turbines could be built. But the embargo also banned the reexport of U.S. goods, and that meant that not even the first six turbines could be shipped to the Soviet Union without breaking the embargo. In addition, JBE

needed communication of technological data from GE in order
to validate GE's performance guarantee. Such data were also
embargoed.

JBE had several options. It could get the rotors elsewhere and make the turbines, change the Soviet contract in
some way so as to at least partially fulfill it, break the
contract, or get the embargo lifted. The options can be outlined as follows:[14]

1.  Buy the rotors from Alsthom Atlantique, the French com-
    pany that had a license from GE to make them, and build
    the turbines with those rotors.
2.  Make the rotors in-house (which was technologically pos-
    sible).
3.  Change the method of pumping gas through the pipeline,
    such as by using some gas turbines and some steam tur-
    bines powered by heat recovered from the gas turbines,
    and change the Soviet contract accordingly.
4.  Make and deliver six turbines using rotors in hand and
    default on the balance of the contract.
5.  Break the entire Soviet contract, or get the Soviets
    jointly to break it, and thus comply with the U.S. em-
    bargo.
6.  Try to get the embargo lifted so that business could pro-
    ceed as usual, or at least lighten its impact.

In considering these options, three background features
affected JBE decision making. First, the company had time
on its side. The embargo came on December 29, 1981, and the
first six turbine deliveries were scheduled for late summer
1982, eight months distant (and six rotors were on hand);
the remaining 15 turbines were due to be delivered in spring
1983, 15 months away. Second, surprising as the embargo was,
nobody in Britain thought it would last very long; hastily
imposed, expeditiously removed was the hope. Third, JBE itself had no U.S. business to speak of, but other John Brown
companies certainly did. There did not appear to be much
genuine U.S. business support for the embargo (U.S. businesses were being hurt as well), but relationships between
John Brown PLC and U.S. business would be an imponderable.[15]

A common response to trade controls is to avoid the
controls by substituting another country's or company's

product. The substitute will never match the original (or it would have been chosen in the first place), but it usually is a plausible short-term solution. Unfortunately for JBE, it was not a solution in this case.

Alsthom Atlantique, which was equipped to make the GE rotor, was under contract only to make spare rotors for the pipeline. Their first rotor was scheduled for completion in late 1983, nearly two years away from JBE's decision point. The French government was pressing Alsthom Atlantique not to give the appearance of contravening the U.S. embargo and, in any event, a large new investment would have been necessary to meet an expanded and accelerated production schedule. JBE would have fallen behind in its contract obligations, probably even if it had used the six GE rotors in hand and thus would have violated the U.S. embargo. This could have triggered a penalty of millions of pounds. JBE would also have had to cancel its order for 15 more GE rotors, with unknown consequences for that essential business relationship. The prospect of getting rotors from Alsthom Atlantique in time was very remote and the costs very high, so this first option had to be rejected. (See Table 12.6 for a summary of the options and their costs and benefits.)

JBE had the technological ability to make the 15 rotors itself but the rotors would first have to be reverse-engineered since JBE did not possess specifications. Then the plant would have to be tooled up. The total investment in money and time would have been huge and quite impractical. Deliveries of turbines to the Soviet Union would have been late, the U.S. embargo would have been violated (unless the six GE rotors were not used), and JBE's manufacturing associate agreement with GE would have been violated, with unknown adverse legal and financial consequences. This "do-it-yourself" option could only have been part of a long-term and permanent shift in the company's business. But what would happen after the Soviet contract was completed? The Soviet-bound turbine was one of five sizes and types; there is just not enough turbine business in the world to warrant JBE production of rotors at an economic cost. Scale economies could not be achieved nor technological advances assured. Long-run production economies and short-term costs ruled out the option of JBE's making its own rotors.

TABLE 12.6

Options, Costs, and Benefits for John Brown
Engineering After U.S. Embargoes Imposed

| Options | Costs and Problems | Benefits and Advantages |
|---|---|---|
| 1. Buy rotors from Alsthom Atlantique | Would Alsthom Atlantique agree? <br><br> Late delivery, subject to 5% penalty (£ millions) <br><br> Break U.S. embargo if use six GE rotors <br><br> Cancellation of GE order for 15 rotors | Complete contract, receive full £104 million <br><br> Retain Soviet goodwill |
| 2. Make own rotors in-house | Reverse engineering needed <br><br> Investment in equipment, tooling up <br><br> High-cost rotors due to small scale, loss on contract <br><br> Late delivery, subject to 5% penalty (£ millions) <br><br> Break U.S. embargo if use six GE rotors <br><br> Cancellation of GE order for 15 rotors <br><br> Jeopardize manufacturing associate agreement with GE | Complete contract, receive full £104 million <br><br> Retain Soviet goodwill |
| 3. Change the method of pumping gas and modify Soviet contract | New design and engineering work needed <br><br> All other European turbine makers must cooperate <br><br> Would Soviets agree? <br><br> Late delivery, subject to 5% penalty (£ millions) <br><br> Break U.S. embargo <br><br> Cancellation of GE order for 15 rotors | Retain bulk of pipeline contract |

(continued)

| Options | Costs and Problems | Benefits and Advantages |
|---|---|---|
| 4. Deliver six turbines, default on the remaining 15 | Breach of Soviet contract, subject to penalties and damages<br><br>Loss of bulk of contract revenue, at least £45 million<br><br>Loss of future Soviet business?<br><br>Break U.S. embargo<br><br>Cancellation of GE order for 15 rotors<br><br>Loss of confidence among suppliers and potential customers | Possible partial coverage by Export Credit Guarantee Department |
| 5. Break the entire Soviet contract | Loss of £104 million revenue<br><br>Subject to penalties and damages<br><br>Loss of future Soviet business?<br><br>Disfavor of U.K. government<br><br>Cancellation of GE order for 15 rotors<br><br>Loss of confidence among suppliers and potential customers | Possible partial coverage by Export Credit Guarantee Department<br><br>Comply with U.S. embargo |
| 6. Seek to get embargo lifted or lightened | Administrative and legal costs<br><br>Inexperienced in political activity; could this succeed? | Complete contract, receive full £104 million<br><br>Retain Soviet goodwill<br><br>Retain GE goodwill |

Source: Compiled and interpreted by the author from sources at John Brown Engineering, John Brown PLC, U.K. government, and press reports.

The next idea was for all the European contractors to agree jointly on a revised method of pumping the natural gas through the pipeline, using the rotors on hand in all the companies (they had 23 out of the required 125) to make gas-fired turbines, and then driving steam turbines via heat recovery from these gas turbines. This, plus the use of some Soviet-made turbines, might get the job done. The European contractors held a meeting in Köln, but the idea went no further. Even if this solution had been adopted, it would have left JBE with many of the problems of the other options--late deliveries, a violation of the U.S. embargo, and cancellation of the GE order. Uncertainty about Soviet cooperation coupled with "half a loaf" of contract revenue vanquished this option.

And so it seemed there was no way of avoiding the U.S. embargo by substitution. The embargo was effective. Either the Soviet contract would have to be broken or the embargo would have to be lifted.

The costs of simply scrapping the Soviet contract would have been staggering: loss of the £104 million in contract revenues; probable penalty levies (5 percent of the contract) and severe consequential damages; possible loss of future Soviet business; loss of an unquantified number of jobs in an already-depressed area; disfavor of the British government (the company is a leading exporter in a trade-dependent nation); and perhaps future problems with GE. It is not an exaggeration to conclude that breaking the contract would have threatened the very survival of JBE.

In return for suffering these costs, JBE would get two benefits. It would be in compliance with the U.S. embargo, but the value of that was uncertain and probably small. The second benefit would have been possible partial reimbursement for losses from the U.K. Export Credit Guarantee Department (ECGD). The U.K. ECGD, which has a function similar to that of the U.S. Export-Import Bank, insures British firms' export sales against nonpayment by the foreign customer (in this case V/O Machinoimport). The coverage is limited to 85 percent of the contract value and to actual costs and expenditures of the contractor. It does not include damage suits or loss of profit. If JBE had been unable to perform on its contract because of interference by a third government (a force majeure such as the U.S. embargo), then

JBE might have been partially compensated. But the export credit guarantee is normally triggered by the <u>customer's</u> nonpayment whereas, in this case, the problem was the <u>seller's</u>. There were no precedents for such a case and no way of putting odds on receiving such a benefit.

Because of the high costs of breaking the Soviet pipeline contract, and because there were eight months before the first contract obligation fell due, JBE decided to continue production, at least for the moment. The one remaining option was to try to get the embargo lifted or lightened.

Can one medium-sized British company, inexperienced in U.S. politics, exert any influence on the U.S. government? Could all the European companies with Soviet pipeline business, acting in concert, make a difference? What is a private-sector company to do in such a case? What, in fact, did JBE do?

What John Brown Engineering Did

JBE did not expect to overturn the U.S. embargo that threatened it. The company's aim was more modest. The decision process was one of reviewing the political issues and assessing the business options in the case, and then of following a consistent policy noteworthy for being low-profile and focused on a political solution. Later on, however, JBE initiated legal proceedings. During all this time, GE obeyed the embargo strictly. No parts and no data for Soviet-bound turbines were shipped.

A delegation of JBE executives that visited Washington, D.C., only days after the U.S. action was officially recorded in the <u>Federal Register</u> of January 5, 1982, took the first step. Their mission was threefold:

1. To clarify the U.S. action with officials at the Departments of Commerce and State. The British Embassy in Washington assisted by identifying the appropriate officials and arranging meetings. Clarification meant establishing that only JBE was affected. John Brown Engineering is a legal entity separate from John Brown PLC, so that only JBE and not John Brown PLC or any other John Brown operating company should be covered by the embargo.

Clarification also meant establishing that only JBE's Soviet oil and gas industry business was affected (not turbines for power generation for other countries).

2. To explain how the U.S. action affected JBE and sketch the implications of special interest to the United States. For example, it would be of interest to the U.S. government to know that JBE had large contracts with Abu Dhabi and Oman for power generation turbines; the United States would not want to displease these governments by interfering with JBE's ability to fulfill those contracts.

3. To get advice from U.S. legal experts on how to proceed further in response to the embargo.

The company also made these views known to the British government officially through the Department of Trade. The government took an active interest at the highest levels (including the Prime Minister) and lodged an official protest with the United States. There was, however, no collusion between the company and the British government, and there was never any jointly planned strategy.

Further JBE actions became apparent later when U.S. sanctions were applied to violators of the embargoes. These were actions of influence, not just clarification. The first violation of the U.S. embargoes was by Dresser-France (which had compressor station contracts) in August 1982. The U.S. sanctions against Dresser-France were broad in scope, but the U.S. denial order against JBE in September 1982 was limited to oil and gas industry applications, not touching applications to other industries. (Subsequently the denial order against Dresser-France was modified and limited in the same way.) This favorable (relatively) treatment of JBE reflected the political efforts of the company and many other people over the preceding months.

Finally, once the denial order was received, JBE requested a formal hearing at the U.S. Department of Commerce, and formal legal discovery procedures were set in motion. JBE's principal argument was that the U.S. embargo was retroactive. The JBE contract had been made three months before the embargo, after a check in the United States about the question of export licenses. While an embargo on future JBE business with the Soviet Union would no doubt have been opposed by JBE, it would have been understood and possibly accepted.

The second point made by JBE was that it had a legally binding contract freely entered into, and that no government, least of all the United States, should erode this essential foundation of free enterprise. The argument was both one of principle--the inviolability of private contracts--and one of practice--the likelihood of extreme economic damage to the company if it had to default on its contract.

The company stressed that it was not taking issue with Washington's foreign policy views about martial law in Poland. Nevertheless, the John Brown group of companies said, "It is a source of great sadness to your directors that this, the most difficult problem facing the company today, should originate in the U.S. where we have invested so significantly in recent years and by doing so have shown, rightly, such confidence in the great contribution that our American companies and colleagues can make to the affairs of this company."16

## The British Directive and the U.S. Sanctions

Between January and June 1982, events in Poland did not improve, U.S.-Soviet relations remained cold, and the pipeline issue was not resolved. Meanwhile, JBE continued to build six turbines for the Soviet Union, hoping that the leaders of the major industrial countries would find a solution to the controversy at the June economic summit in Versailles.

It did not happen. President Reagan thought he got a concession from the Europeans, at least on the issue of soft export credits for the East, but President Mitterand promptly repudiated any such deal, and misunderstanding ruled. The second U.S. embargo, now including foreign subsidiaries and licensees of U.S. firms, was imposed on June 18, 1982.

While the second embargo had no further effect on JBE or the other European turbine makers (except for Alsthom Atlantique, they were neither subsidiaries nor licensees), the British and European governments were outraged by the extraterritoriality of this extension. On June 30, the British government declared that its trading interests were damaged. On August 2, it directed JBE and three other British firms not to comply with the U.S. embargoes, using Section 1 of the U.K. Protection of Trading Interests Act of

1980 for the first time.[17]  The government then made it
quite clear that JBE was expected to obey British law, not
U.S. law, or else it would face unspecified financial penalties.  It was also made clear that there would be no government compensation to JBE because of losses suffered due to
the directive.

If before there had been little chance to avoid breaking the U.S. embargo, now there was no way out.  There was
no thought of violating the British directive, and JBE announced it would meet its first contractual obligation to
ship six turbines to the Soviet Union.  The U.S. sanctions
followed once the Clydebank docks were cleared and the Soviet
ship departed.  If these sanctions were effective and stuck,
JBE would be cut off from GE rotors destined for oil and gas
industry use and at least temporarily limited to GE rotors
for power generation use.  Because the U.S. denial order was
anticipated, there was time for JBE to influence the order
so as to leave JBE's power generation business (historically
the larger share) untouched.  (Some sources claim the U.S.
government was sympathetic.)  Nevertheless, JBE resorted to
legal proceedings.  The economic consequences were scarcely
calculable.

Just over two months later, the United States lifted
the sanctions and embargoes, but the classic happy ending is
still not in sight.  The sanctions did long-term damage and
altered Anglo-American trade relations.  The problem of extraterritoriality confounding international trade still has
not been solved.

As to the net cost of this episode to John Brown PLC,
no figure was ever mentioned.  The situation was too fluid.
The company did not know how much business it was never given
a chance to bid on because the Soviets were not confident
the firm could deliver.  It also had no idea how much staff
time and indirect cost it incurred.  The company did what it
thought it had to do to save its business.[18]  (On February
28, 1983, JBE announced it was invited to bid on a new £16
million contract to supply gas turbines for another Soviet-
Czechoslovakian natural gas pipeline.  A month earlier, another unit of John Brown, Wickman Ltd., won an order for £4
million worth of machine tools for the Soviet Union.)

## THE LESSONS OF THE PIPELINE CONTROVERSY

This case had no winners.  U.S. firms suffered, but not JBE, the British government, or any European companies or governments would claim to be winners.  Whenever there are no winners (except perhaps the Soviet Union) and only losers, opportunities to do better next time are assured.

This case is also one in which a trade control worked-- in the sense that it could not be evaded at reasonable cost. Ironically, because it worked so well in the short run, but had such great long-run economic and political costs, it could not last.

The 1982 Soviet gas pipeline case is not yet over. JBE's contractual obligations will not be completed until 1987 due to the spare parts and service provisions of its contract.  In the meantime, new cases such as the pipeline controversy are bound to arise, and new legislation and court tests appear inevitable, but the governments have not yet conducted the discussions that need to follow from the deal that led to the lifting of the U.S. embargoes.

Those discussions need to take place to prevent or at least minimize future disagreements on trade controls.  When they do take place, the participants would do well to study the lessons learned from the JBE case.  There are plenty of lessons to be learned from this case, including lessons for business policy, business-government relations, and public policy.


Foreign Trade Policy Differences Between
the United States and Great Britain

Perhaps the most important NATO-related lesson is that the United States and Great Britain (and the Europeans) have fundamentally different views of the role of trade in international relations.  The Soviet gas pipeline controversy is only the latest in a long series of foreign trade policy differences between the United States and Britain, particularly over the extraterritoriality issue.  These differences stem in part from fundamentally different views about foreign trade in the two countries.

First, foreign trade is much more important to Britain than to the United States. Exports amounted to 27 percent of Britain's gross domestic product in 1981 (second only to Holland among industrialized countries); in the United States the figure is less than 10 percent, although it is rising. The British economy is dependent on foreign trade for its well-being. To make matters worse, British trade with the Soviet Union runs a substantial deficit, and the British share of total exports to the COMECON countries has been dropping. In contrast, U.S. firms have been gaining an increasing share of engineering exports to those countries.[19] All of this background makes JBE exports to the USSR that much more important.

Second, the British government does not, as a rule, believe in the use of foreign trade as an instrument of foreign policy, especially in peacetime. Quite practically, Britain does not have the capability to do so, not having possessed either world economic dominance or technological monopolies for many years. The United States does possess this capability and has mixed trade policy and foreign policy. The identification of trade policy with foreign policy continues in the United States, although some observers now doubt Washington's capability in this realm. Of course, the United States needs, more than Britain does, to use all available weapons in the conduct of its foreign policy as long as it continues its dominant role in the military defense of Europe.

British criticism of some aspects of U.S. foreign trade policy is unofficially virulent. The policy is charged with being changeable and unpredictable--"lightswitch" diplomacy-- and is thought to be inconsistent, hypocritical, and commercially motivated (e.g., the United States sells wheat to the USSR to aid American agriculture while it tries to block sales of gas turbines to the USSR by Europeans).[20] The British believe the policy is laden with controls and regulations, and the British government dislikes Washington's perceived unilateral "go-it-alone" tendency; they would like to be included more often.

The issues and problems in the 1982 Soviet gas pipeline case emerged from these long-standing policy differences and latent discontents. The way out of the problem must accordingly take them into account.

The Business Decision Process

The JBE case also provides lessons for businesses caught in a political cross-fire. The reaction of JBE suggests one approach other businesses might consider. (As in any case study, these policies are to some extent situation-specific, and other companies in other cases might behave differently.)

The first thing JBE did was to ask what the political-- and moral--issues in the case were. Quite clearly JBE did not like and did not agree with the U.S. embargoes and sanctions, but the company could understand that President Reagan had to do something about the events in Poland and that adverse fallout in Europe (if it was anticipated at all) was easier for him to live with than the domestic consequences of doing nothing. So at least a minimum of political awareness is a prerequisite for companies.

The second thing that JBE did was to outline the business options available and to assess them. JBE could do this quickly and decisively. The embargo could not be evaded except at too high a cost. Making the turbine rotors in-house was economically (not technologically) impractical. Getting the rotors from Alsthom Atlantique might have been possible, but only as a last resort. No matter which business option JBE chose, they had to aim for a strategy of minimizing losses. In any event, they emphasized their determination to honor their contract. "The John Brown board has always taken the view that we have a duty to make every effort possible to meet fully our commitments under this internationally binding contract which was entered into in good faith some three months before the U.S. government instituted its embargo. . . ."[21]

Third, JBE adopted a political strategy to cope with a political problem. The political strategy included three policy approaches: a low profile with low-key actions such as minimum press contact (during the 11 months of the case there were only five press releases from the company); no statements of actions to inflame U.S. government officials who, it was hoped, would recant the embargoes; and informal and quiet discussions with influential policymakers in the United States and Britain. It is this sort of approach that can tell a company that there is little U.S. business support for the embargo and some desire even on the part of the U.S. government to find a way out of the problem.

No medium-sized company can by itself change a government's policy, but a company can facilitate a change, and that requires the company to act politically.


## The Issues and the Way Ahead

### The Cost of Trade Barriers

The U.S. export embargo, which lasted 320 days, will have effects on international business that will last much longer. The aggregate economic loss from the temporary trade barrier will continue because of the expectation of other trade controls in the future. In other words, business firms, taking note of their recent experience, will act as if there were a (perhaps small) trade barrier now in effect because of their positive expectation of one in the future. There must be some doubt lingering in customers' minds about the ability of companies to perform contracts using U.S. equipment or technology when there is the ever-present risk of U.S. legislation that could cut off the supply of U.S. or U.S.-related goods.

International trade theorists have known since the nineteenth century that whenever there are two countries such that each has a cost advantage in the production of one commodity (comparative as well as absolute advantage), then trade between them will be profitable for both. If General Electric can make turbine rotors better or cheaper than European firms, then any artificial barrier to trade in rotors will raise the cost of aggregate output in both the United States and Europe. In this case, there are clear examples of the costs of trade barriers.

The clear losers from the U.S. embargoes are U.S. firms with international business, such as General Electric, and British and European firms that use U.S. products or services, such as JBE. This is why a European consortium of firms now becomes a serious prospect to replace U.S. sources of high-technology, large-scale products, even if their products may cost more. JBE has not yet made any changes in its manufacturing associate agreement with GE, and John Brown PLC as a group has not made any changes in its investment in

U.S. business, but trade between U.S. and European companies has surely been diminished by the Soviet pipeline case. Even though the public may not care about the profits of GE or JBE in particular, the public surely does care about overall cost of output.

The business policy lesson that is regrettably learned from the Soviet gas pipeline case is that the risk premium of trading with U.S. companies in products or services at all connected with U.S. foreign policy must be increased. U.S. companies must accordingly work harder to maintain their previous trade levels.

The second policy lesson is that trade controls raise costs for the imposer of the controls as well as for the object of the controls. These costs were apparent in this case, and they will always occur. Furthermore, the costs will occur in the long run and well as in the present. Lifting the trade control does not erase all its costs.

## Retroactivity

The first U.S. export embargo in this case was imposed three months after JBE signed its contracts to make turbines for the Soviet Union and buy rotors from GE. The embargo occurred despite JBE's inquiries with governments about the rotor transaction and despite the fact that the company had a valid preexisting business contract. How can international trade occur in an environment in which contracts are not secure? When a government can, with one simple unforeseen stroke, overturn a legal business agreement, what are the future prospects for business trade deals? Of course not all foreign trade occurs over long contract time periods-- not all companies and not all trade are exposed to the kind of problems that JBE and GE suffered--and political events of great importance may require policy steps to be taken by governments.

The source of the ever-present conflict is the need for business to depend on valid foreign contracts versus the need for governments to respond to adverse foreign events. The conflict, however, is neither inevitable nor irreducible. One solution is to lessen the use of foreign trade as a foreign policy weapon (using other means instead) or to avoid retroactive sanctions. Such a change might, according to some Americans, diminish the potency of U.S. foreign policy.

Another solution is for the United States to consult with
its allies more before imposing retroactive trade controls
in order to assess the economic costs of doing so before the
fact and before a mistake is made.

## U.S. Objectives

The retroactivity issue was worsened by British uncertainty about what the U.S. objectives were for the export
embargoes.  Several different objectives appeared at different times:

1. Prevent the pipeline from being built because Western
   Europe would become too dependent on Soviet natural gas
   and thus hostage to Soviet foreign policy.  (According
   to the Economist, 15 percent of Europe's natural gas was
   imported in 1982; the figure was forecast to rise to 36
   percent by 1990, and Soviet gas would be 23 percent of
   total consumption.)[22]
2. Deny the USSR hard-currency earnings as part of a more
   general strategy of economic warfare at a time when the
   Soviet Union's economy was thought to be weak, and thus
   reduce the Soviet military build-up and make her more
   compliant.
3. Punish the USSR for complicity with the imposition of
   martial law in Poland and thereby seek to force a liber-
   alization in Poland.
4. Prevent the transfer of critical technology to the USSR
   in the belief that most of the Soviet Union's advanced
   technology had been simply purchased from the West and
   that this was an opportunity to reverse this undesirable
   trend.
5. Force a change in the subsidy from European countries to
   the Soviet Union that arose from the below-market interest rates on the export credits granted along with the
   sale of pipeline equipment.

The timing of the first U.S. embargo--enacted just
after martial law was imposed in Poland--suggested the third
objective of punishing the USSR for that political event,
and indeed that objective was cited in the embargo itself.
Had any of the other economic objectives prevailed, the U.S.
export embargo could have been announced well in advance of

any East-West business deals and the retroactivity problem avoided. The United States had opposed the European purchase of Soviet gas in the first place, but as time passed and further U.S. statements were made, these other objectives appeared operative, especially when the second embargo was imposed and diplomatic discussions increasingly involved questions of high-technology trade and soft export credits.

The problem is simply that when the (unintended) target of attack does not know why it is being aggrieved, it does not know how to repel the attack. The lesson is simply that a more clear-cut U.S. position all along could have eased negotiations and reduced the damage done.

## Extraterritoriality

The Soviet pipeline case is a clear example of jurisdictional conflict between governments. The U.S. Export Administration Act of 1979 empowers the U.S. Department of Commerce to impose trade controls for national security or foreign policy reasons on U.S. companies, products, or services and on foreign companies controlled by U.S. interests. The odious parts of this act for British companies and the British government are the "foreign policy reasons" and the coverage of non-U.S. enterprise. Under this act a British-registered and located company is subject to U.S. law if it uses U.S.-originated products or services or has a controlling U.S. ownership (which in some cases involves as little as 25 percent ownership of the equity). Thus the reach of the U.S. law is very long and very broad, and it appears to have no parallel among the trading nations of the world.

The British, however, have a law of their own, the Protection of Trading Interests Act of 1980, under which the Department of Trade can direct a British-registered company not to obey a foreign government if Britain's trading interests would be damaged. A business firm can then find itself in the impossible dilemma of choosing whose law to obey and whose law to violate, as JBE did, suffering penalties no matter which way it turned. Clearly an intergovernmental resolution of the extraterritoriality issue is required, via modifications to national legislation or international legal opinion. The British government attaches great importance to this. In its opinion, extraterritoriality continues to be the worst problem in U.S.-British commercial relations, and has been so for over 20 years.

## Export Credits

There are two separate issues about export credits in foreign trade. The first, of special interest to the business firm, is the question of guaranteeing payment to the exporter and insuring it against risk of loss. One of the reasons for quasi-governmental bankers and insurers who arrange financing and guarantee payment by the buyer on behalf of the exporter is the political risk of many trade deals. But in this case, it was not known if JBE could have been compensated for any economic losses it would have suffered had the U.S. embargo continued. To make matters worse, once JBE was ordered by the British government not to comply with the U.S. embargo, the company's ECGD coverage could have been in jeopardy. Because of recent claims against it, the ECGD is narrowing its coverage (i.e., excluding losses arising from the actions of the U.S. government) and raising its premium. What businesses need, at a minimum, is better advance knowledge of the terms and conditions of export credit guarantees, lest a further diminution in foreign trade occurs.

The second issue regarding export credits is the interest rate at which they are provided. In the case of the Soviet gas pipeline, the borrowing rates were below market and thus constituted a subsidy to the Soviet Union. Many countries do not want their export competitiveness tied to their domestic borrowing rates--which depend on internal phenomena such as price inflation, money supply growth, and government budget deficits--and so a consensus export finance rate is determined internationally in the OECD. That rate at the time of the Soviet pipeline deal was about 8.5 percent, whereas British international borrowing rates were about 13.5 percent. The Soviets got the 8.5 percent rate, and the difference was made up by the British government. (Of course a credit subsidy at one time could be a credit tax at another time if internal rates were lower than the international rate.)

Should the consensus export credit rate mechanism continue to be used as it is at present? Should that rate be variable according to the buyer and project? These are questions for intergovernmental resolution with the aid of business opinion.

## Consultation and the Role of International Organizations

The first U.S. embargo on December 29, 1981, was a surprise to the British government as well as to JBE.  The news came via the morning newspapers.  The second embargo was equally undisclosed in advance.  There were no trial balloons, there was no joint discussion of joint ways and means to achieve U.S. objectives toward the Soviet Union, even though some of these objectives were shared.  Of course, bilateral consultation takes time, and multilateral consultation takes more time, but repairing damage from lack of consultation also takes time.  The success that JBE had in limiting the scope of the U.S. embargoes and sanctions—the return the company seemed to get from explaining the consequences of the U.S. action ex post—suggest that ex ante consultation could have averted the crisis.

There are international organizations for consultation and joint problem solving.  The OECD can serve, both through its export credit rate-setting facility and through COCOM.  Although COCOM is not part of OECD, its function is to list products and technologies embargoed for export from West to East and to make exceptions to its own list.  The rotors and turbines in this case were not on the COCOM list, so there was no COCOM involvement, but more consultation about the export credit terms for East-West trade and about what constitutes high technology to be embargoed must take place in the future.  A further accommodation is required on the role of trade in East-West politics so that private-sector businesses have a framework within which to operate and so that foreign trade can thrive to everyone's gain.

NOTES

1.  Angela Stent Yergin, East-West Technology Transfers: European Perspectives, Washington Papers, vol. 8, no. 75 (Beverly Hills and London:  Sage Publications, 1980).

2.  John Brown Engineering Ltd., "Gas Turbine Experience Summary," and "The Industrial Gas Turbine," Clydebank, Scotland.

3.  Ibid.

4.  John Brown Engineering Ltd., "Press Release," October 13, 1981.

5.  Ibid.

6.  Ibid.

7.  U.S. Federal Register, vol. 47, no. 2 (January 5, 1982), p. 145.

8.  Ibid., p. 144.

9.  Federal Register, vol. 47, no. 122 (June 24, 1982).

10.  United Kingdom Department of Trade, "Press Notice," August 2, 1982.

11.  John Brown PLC, "News Release," August 2, 1982.

12.  United Kingdom Department of Trade, "Press Notice," September 10, 1982.

13.  Malcolm R. Hill, East-West Trade, Industrial Co-operation and Technology Transfer:  The British Experience (Aldershot, England:  Gower Press, 1983).

14.  The information in this and the following section is based on several industry and government sources and press reports.  What follows, however, is a model constructed by the author and reflecting his views.

15.  Caterpillar stood to lose $90 million and General Electric $175 million in revenue.

16.  John Brown PLC, Annual Report 1982, p. 6.

17.  United Kingdom Department of Trade, "Press Notice, August 2, 1982.

18.  On February 28, 1983, JBE announced it was invited to bid on a new £16 million contract to supply gas turbines for another Soviet-Czechoslovakian natural gas pipeline.  A month earlier, another unit of John Brown, Wickman Ltd., won an order for sales of machine tools for the Soviet Union.

19.  Hill, 1983.

20.  The United States argued that wheat is a consumption good that drains the Soviet Union of scarce foreign currency reserves while gas turbines are an investment good that will earn foreign exchange for the Soviets.  Another example is the U.S. cooperation with the UN-sponsored boycott

of Rhodesia when it came to tobacco (no Rhodesian imports meant less competitors for southern U.S. farmers), coupled with the U.S. noncooperation when it came to chrome (which was needed for the U.S. military).

21.   John Brown PLC, "News Release," August 2, 1982.

22.   Economist, July 10, July 17, and July 31, 1982.

# 13

# THE IMPLEMENTATION OF TRADE SANCTIONS

## Leonard Santos

This chapter discusses the implementation of trade sanctions, and it should be stated at the outset that, in the experience of this writer, trade sanctions have become exercises in symbolism. Thus, there is little hope that their implementation or their costs are likely to weigh heavily in future deliberations on their use unless a more hard-headed approach is adopted. This chapter will return to the symbolic nature of many recent trade sanctions after discussing the implementation of the most recent use of trade sanctions—the Siberian natural gas pipeline export controls.

The description in earlier chapters of the cost that Fiatallis and JBE paid in connection with the Soviet pipeline affair reminds one that those costs were largely ignored in deciding to use this economic weapon. Indeed, some of those costs might have been avoided if the decision to limit exports associated with the Siberian pipeline had been preceded by a careful assessment of the prospects for implementation.

---

AUTHOR'S NOTE: The opinions expressed in this article are the views of the author and do not necessarily reflect the views of the Senate Finance Committee.

One of the curious aspects of the pipeline sanctions is that although the decision to impose them was an expression of U.S. policy toward the Soviet Union, the implementation of that decision became a matter of international economic policy. The cabinet-level group for international economic policy, known as the SIG-IEP (Senior Interagency Group for International Economic Policy), assumed responsibility for the postdecision implementation that ended in a revocation of the sanctions. The fact that the sanctions ultimately were withdrawn suggests that the SIG-IEP, chaired by the Treasury Department, developed a new and different assessment of the utility of the pipeline sanctions. That such an assessment was not developed prior to the pipeline decisions says more about the shifting influence of key decisionmakers than about what facts might have been available to them.

One fact that emerged clearly after the sanctions were imposed and that could have been anticipated was the strenuous resistance of the Europeans to the extraterritorial imposition of pipeline export controls. Although the decisionmakers had been informed of the perils of the extraterritoriality, nothing could emphasize this point like the reaction of the Europeans, particularly France and the United Kingdom.

Several countries took actions specifically to countermand the dictates of U.S. export controls, something that had not happened in a dramatic way since the mid-1960s, when the United States tried to prevent a sale by a French company to the Chinese. It had not been dramatized to senior people that the essential problem with extraterritoriality is that it does not work. The Soviet pipeline incident was useful from that point of view. It dramatized for those people, in a way no memorandum possibly could, that extraterritorial export controls, at least when they are being used against companies of our major trading partners, are not going to work. They are not going to work because those countries object, as a matter of principle, to the extension of jurisdiction, and they have passed laws or have the capability to pass laws that authorize them to countermand the sanctions. Unless the United States is prepared to declare war on its allies or do some other extravagant thing to them, the story ends there. The story ends when the French marshals accompany a shipment to Le Havre to ensure that it is put on board a ship destined for the Soviet Union, contrary to U.S. controls. That is the bottom line when one is talking about extraterritoriality. The United States does not have it within its power to prevent their exportation.

Another fact to emerge following the pipeline decision related to the terms of contracts signed between GE and several of the key European pipeline suppliers. The Wall Street Journal and others suggested that clauses in those GE contracts requiring the European suppliers to comply with U.S. export controls provided the United States with a means of enforcing extraterritorial export controls. It took some time after the pipeline decision to conclude that those clauses gave the United States (as opposed to GE) no additional leverage over the European exports in question. The point of this is that if implementation of the pipeline sanctions had been assessed as carefully before as after the decision, a different decision might have been reached.

Following the pipeline sanctions decision, some thought was given to the potential economic hardship that would be inflicted on European companies if the United States issued sweeping punitive orders against violators of its export controls. Information started to filter from U.S. allies about the damage that would be incurred if the United States started issuing broad punitive orders of the sort then being considered. The sober reality of pushing companies of friendly governments into bankruptcy helped to modify and narrow the terms of the denial orders.

Ironically, for all the concern over the European companies affected by the denial orders, little attention was given to the indirect costs incurred by U.S. companies. Would foreign companies avoid future reliance on U.S. suppliers because of the unpredictable propensity of the U.S. government to use trade sanctions? Would U.S. companies pay a heavy price in lost sales to the USSR, only to have that market filled by European and Japanese competitors? These are questions that received little attention either before or after the imposition of the pipeline sanctions.

A point to be made about the implementation of trade sanctions in general is that implementation becomes almost irrelevant as the sanctions become symbolic. During the

Carter administration, trade sanctions often were used to "send a signal," particularly in the human rights area. Increasingly, it has become fashionable to propose trade sanctions as a signal of U.S. resolve, outrage, disapproval, or whatever.  In many of these cases, the use of trade sanctions is not expected to achieve any particular result other than to provide tangible evidence of U.S. policy.  Without addressing the value of signaling a principled foreign policy, one can wonder about the location of the receivers picking up these signals.  Surely the receivers are not located in the countries whose exporters are quick to exploit the void created by U.S. export controls.  Nor have the signals seemed to impress the targets of export controls, such as the Soviet Union and South Africa.  But the fact that trade sanctions are used as a means of sending a signal makes it easier to disregard their costs and their feasibility.

Unfortunately, one can rarely quantify what concrete results are produced through the sending of signals other than some sort of better feeling about one's decisiveness in a particular situation.  And that, after all, is what economic sanctions have become.  They have become the course of least resistance between, on the one hand, declaring war or getting into an armed conflict and, on the other hand, delivering a weak diplomatic protest.  They are a nice middle ground in which the appearance of decision and the appearance of action substitute for accomplishing any particular goal.

Another point to be made about the implementation of trade sanctions is that they are more effective when they are adopted multilaterally.  It is an obvious point, but one that cannot be overstated.  For example, U.S. allies agreed on limited trade sanctions against Iran, and it was our experience, as we sat through the morning briefings from intelligence officers at the Treasury Department, that our allies tried, to the greatest extent possible, to keep the United States happy and still continue doing business with Iran. In some cases, it was clearly an official government policy to wink and look the other way.  In other cases, it was just plain old sloppiness in enforcing trade sanctions. But it was clear that, in the Iran trade sanctions case, very few of the allies enforced trade sanctions to the extent to which they had agreed.

In that case, the President chose to freeze Iranian bank assets, both in the United States and in overseas branches of U.S. banks. When it came to the use of trade sanctions, he was advised that he should not attempt to enforce trade sanctions extraterritorially. Instead, there would be a so-called jawboning policy, whereby the U.S. companies would persuade their foreign subsidiaries not to sell the goods that they themselves could not sell to Iran. The United States sent a mission over to the European Economic Community and to Japan to obtain their cooperation in the enforcement of trade sanctions. These countries did agree to a limited number of trade sanctions because they preferred that to a U.S. blockade of the Gulf of Hormuz, which would interrupt their oil supplies. We thought we had their agreement, but during the 18 months that those sanctions were in place, they were routinely violated, and although those sanctions may have put great pressure on Iran, their effectiveness was more a reflection of Iran's relatively weak and dependent situation. If the target had been the Soviet Union and the same amount of leakage had occurred, it is doubtful that the sanctions would have had much of an impact. So the lesson is that multilateral export controls are generally a better solution, but their effectiveness can be undermined by lax multilateral enforcement and they may result in foreign competitors getting the advantage over U.S. exporters.

A final point about the implementation of trade sanctions: statutorily prescribed procedural requirements do not effectively limit the use of trade sanctions. Someone recited the terms of the Export Administration Act, which requires that findings be made before foreign policy export controls can be applied. There are similar kinds of requirements in statutes such as the International Emergency Economic Powers Act, which was the basis for the Iran sanctions. Such findings have little if any utility. They do not restrain or limit presidents, because they are simply too easily manufactured. They do not represent any real limitation on a president's power to impose export controls or other kinds of trade sanctions.

As an example of the liberties that presidents take, one can cite President Carter's reliance on his national security export control authority to impose the Soviet grain embargo. Presumably, President Carter relied on his national security authority to avoid the relatively mechanical task of making the finding required of foreign policy export controls. Presidents find ways to do what they want to do, and if the statutes are written in a sufficiently vague or discretionary manner, they will use that discretion and they will take advantage of the vagueness. Basically, the decision is made when the authority is delegated by Congress. Beyond that, none of these procedural constraints that are written into the Export Administration Act and other statutes does much other than create a lot of paperwork.

It has not been the intention of this chapter to discount totally the utility of trade sanctions. Rather, it has tried to highlight the drift toward using trade sanctions for symbolic purposes. These sanctions have been overused, in many cases to the substantial detriment of our economic interests. No country, even one as rich as the United States, can long afford to trample on its trading relationships casually and without obtaining some tangible advantage. One step in relearning self-restraint is to avoid sanctions that cannot be implemented.

# IV

# DEVELOPING A MORE EFFECTIVE EXPORT CONTROL POLICY

As the final section in the book, Part IV examines ways to build reasonable commercial ties with political adversaries. The section contains five chapters, each of which discusses some specific proposals to improve either the legislation for or the implementation of export controls.

Congressman Don Bonker leads off the section with a discussion of the debate over the Export Administration Act. He argues in favor of the bill developed by the House Foreign Affairs Committee, although he agrees that there are some problems in the bill. In general, Bonker supports changes that would relieve U.S. businesses of some of the burdens of trade restrictions. He also spends some time discussing the debate over the legislation in Congress, providing some valuable insight into the legislative process.

Senator John Heinz provides a Senate view of the Export Administration Act renewal debate. Heinz discusses the Senate bill, the House bill, and the administration bill in his chapter. He argues that the Senate bill is the only one that successfully balances the need to export and the need to control some trade. Heinz argues that the House bill, while a good attempt, leans too far toward exports and, at the same time, deals exporters a critical blow through its contract sanctity clause.

Paul Freedenberg, in the next chapter, looks specifically at the high-technology provisions of the Senate bill to renew the Export Administration Act. Freedenberg investigates the two premises with which the Senate Banking Committee worked when it formulated the bill: the premise that the Soviets, under Yuri Andropov, are engaged in a major effort to obtain Western military technology and the premise that the United States has a monopoly on very few technologies. Freedenberg then examines how the committee attempted to deal with these premises, and he concludes with a study of the controversial import sanction provision of the bill.

Raymond J. Waldmann's chapter looks at one specific and controversial use of trade controls: foreign policy controls. Waldmann examines the rationale behind foreign policy controls and discusses the basis for them in the Export Administration Act. He then studies several proposals to amend the act to improve the use of foreign policy controls, but he concludes that the foreign policy section of the act as it stands now is the best that the country can do. Based on that, he advocates better use of the existing legislation to improve foreign policy controls.

In the final chapter, W. Bruce Weinrod examines the role of national security export controls, and he makes several recommendations to improve such controls. Weinrod argues in favor of multilateral controls and supports U.S. pressure against those countries that choose not to cooperate. He then makes a series of recommendations to improve both unilateral and multilateral national security controls, promoting the use of such controls while acknowledging the need to free U.S. businesses from the handicap of wasteful and unnecessary controls.

# 14

# RECONCILING EXPORT OPPORTUNITIES AND NATIONAL SECURITY POLICY: RENEWAL OF THE EXPORT ADMINISTRATION ACT

## Don Bonker

In dealing with the issue of export controls, the United States must reconcile a serious policy dilemma regarding its strategic and foreign policy objectives. The United States, as one of the two superpowers, must maintain certain standards in terms of technology transfers and the use of economic sanctions to carry out certain foreign policy objectives. These are burdens this country must carry alone, since very few other countries will share in them. At the same time, we should recognize that the U.S. domestic economy is no longer sufficient to meet the country's growth needs. Therefore, in order to experience economic recovery and growth at home, U.S. businesses have to find new outlets for their products.

The question of how to balance these policy imperatives will certainly be the issue when Congress takes up the Export Administration Act. Congress faces a number of controversial provisions in the bill, and these are now exacerbated by the emotional fallout from the Korean Air Lines incident.

The Export Administration Act renewal bill developed in the House Foreign Affairs Committee is fully supported by the business community, and for good reason. It attempts to deal realistically with both the foreign policy and the national security provisions of the act. The committee found, for instance, that foreign policy controls simply

have not worked in the past.  During a meeting with some
European parliamentarian friends, committee members were
reminded that foreign policy controls have never worked, at
least in the recent history of Great Britain, which attempted to utilize sanctions to carry out its own foreign
policy objectives.  The Europeans cautioned that, just as
the British have learned, we will discover that foreign
policy controls do not work, however desirable they might
seem as a policy option.

In the United States' own brief experience, foreign
policy controls certainly have not proved very effective.
They were ineffective both during the Carter administration—when Washington utilized controls on the export of
grain to the Soviet Union—and during the Reagan administration, when the President imposed restrictions on products
to be used in the construction of the Yamal gas pipeline.
In both instances, there was neither the proper consultation
with allies nor the necessary domestic political support to
make those controls effective.  As a result, U.S. businesses have been left in disarray and with a reputation as
questionable suppliers.  They have also lost vast new markets internationally.

In both of these recent cases, the President ultimately lifted the restrictions, but they proved injurious
to the business community during the short time they were
in effect.  Instead of inflicting punishment on the Soviet
Union, the sanctions appear to have hurt the U.S. business
community.  If those controls had worked, if they had
proved to be effective consistently, then there would be a
rationale for keeping them in place.  Some would ask:  "Why
not retain the authority so that the President, in the future, can use economic controls, even if they have proved
ineffective in the past."  The argument against this question is that the authority, as long as it exists, gives
U.S. businesses the reputation as unreliable suppliers.  The
control authority itself enhances that reputation.

The second argument against the use of foreign policy
controls is fairly profound in view of what has just happened.  If there has been a dastardly act by the Soviet
Union in recent years, it has to be the murderous shooting
down of the Korean airliner.  And, if there were reason why
the President ought to punish the Soviet Union by imposing

economic controls under the foreign policy section of the
act, the jetliner incident ought to have been the reason.
Yet this president has learned by his own experience. Despite his own personal concern about the Soviet action and
his compassion for those involved, he stopped short of
resorting to economic controls. If this President did not
use economic controls under these circumstances, it is
doubtful he will do so in the future.

National security controls are a far more complex
issue. They involve technology transfer, and the state of
the art in this area is such that it is terribly difficult
to determine the impact that a technology exported to
various places, East and West, will have on the military
capability of an adversary nation. Any attempt to control
virtually every technology--even if that technology is dated
and even if there is foreign availability--makes it extremely difficult for U.S. manufacturers; it definitely
has been a problem in recent years.

The House bill attempts to tackle this problem by
looking, first of all, at trade between the United States
and its allies--those countries that are member nations of
COCOM, principally the NATO countries plus Japan. It makes
little sense to continue with control requirements or licensing requirements for shipments to very friendly coun-
tries--those that support our efforts strategically and
are members of NATO--so a major reform in the House bill
removes licensing requirements for shipments to COCOM countries. This reform should eliminate about one-third of the
70,000 licenses now required. Also, the House bill attempts
to decontrol unilateral licenses for those items or products
that have been approved for export consistently over the
past year. In other words, if an item has been approved
for export repeatedly and is in international circulation,
it makes no sense to continue the licensing requirement or
to deny export licenses in the future.

The House bill also deals with the problem of foreign
availability. If there is one thing that upsets the international business executive, it is to have a product denied
a license for national security reasons, only to realize
that an overseas competitor does not face similar licensing
requirements. The committee, believing that foreign availability reform is very important, has included in its bill

a provision making it possible for the Technical Advisory
Committee to petition the Secretary of Commerce when it
knows of foreign availability. Beyond that, the reform
would require the Secretary to make a determination of foreign availability. If the availability does exist, the
item would be automatically decontrolled. The decontrol
would come only after the Secretary had a certain amount of
time in which to negotiate with the country where the product is available to bring about a license requirement or
control requirement for that particular commodity. If the
Secretary does not succeed, then the U.S. business executive
will not be punished or denied an opportunity to compete in
that particular market.

Another controversial issue in the debate over the
renewal of the Export Administration Act is contract sanctity. The Senate bill sponsored by Senator Heinz contains
a timely provision on this important issue. Congress already has provided contract sanctity for agricultural and
commodity goods, so there is no reason why it cannot extend
it for manufactured goods as well. The contract sanctity
provision on the House side was compromised by way of the
Berman Amendment--which allows the President to retain
authority to break contracts in cases where countries violate human rights or take certain other actions specified in
the amendment. The contract sanctity provision I support,
however, which is the one now retained in the Senate bill,
is the only way to deal effectively with this problem of
presidential authority on controls. It protects existing
contracts, thereby helping U.S. companies overseas that are
faced with their own dilemma when our country terminates
their contracts for foreign policy considerations while the
resident country has a law that requires them to honor contracts. Congress has added an extraterritoriality provision
to the bill so that, in the future, controls cannot be extended to companies in other countries.

Congress is moving in the right direction, at least
through its committee deliberation, on this section of the
bill. At a minimum, it must insure that, in the future, the
President cannot place controls on existing contracts.

One of the most controversial sections of the House
bill deals with enforcement. The committee has criticized
the Department of Commerce's enforcement performance; there

are many reasons why it has not been as effective as it should be. As a result, the administration has set up another program, known as Operation Exodus, now being funded by the Department of Defense but soon to be funded by a congressional authorization to the Customs Service. This program provides the Customs Service with the authority to conduct random inspections to attempt to locate cargo carrying technology that might be transferred or exported illegally. It has proved to be burdensome to the business community, because Customs lacks the technical expertise to make determinations of what technology is controlled and should be controlled. The result has been many delays and much more red tape involving the possible shipment of certain products or technology.

If there is a problem in enforcement, the solution is to enhance the Department of Commerce's enforcement division to give it the resources necessary to improve its enforcement capability. The answer certainly is not to bring two agencies into enforcement, giving both money and statutory authority to deal with the problem. Such a policy will only add confusion and inefficiency to the system. The committee has attempted to deal with the enforcement problem, in part, by limiting the Customs Service's authority to its more traditional responsibility of tracking illegal exports of technology, and by keeping within the Department of Commerce, with an increased budget, the traditional enforcement authority. That provision may be one of the more controversial parts of the bill because it is one area in which Senators Garn and Heinz have agreed that Customs Service should have not partial but full enforcement authority.

To turn to another aspect of U.S. export control policy, it is interesting to note the direction we are moving with regard to the People's Republic of China. The recent policy changes indicate that this government is willing to differentiate between various socialist governments in its export control policy. During a recent trip to China, I brought the message to the Chinese that the Reagan administration, supported by Congress, is prepared to lift many of the restrictions and to expedite licensing procedures for technology transfer to China. In the past, the United States has placed China in the same category as the Soviet

Union, so very little, if any, technology reached it. The Reagan administration, as a result of Secretary Baldrige's visit to Beijing, has decided to shift China into a new category: one of friendly nations. That symbolic gesture has been made, but it has to be backed by more substantive action. Many members of Congress received a briefing line from the Secretary about the new China policy, and everybody should be pleased with it. It does not compromise our security interests, and it will help to enhance our economic, trade, and political relations with China.

Everywhere the congressional delegation traveled in China, it discovered great enthusiasm for technology. Modernization is one of China's goals for the next decade, and they cannot really modernize, in their industry or anywhere else, until they have mastered technology. They need to develop a computer capability that will make them more efficient in their various modernization goals. The delegation found varying degrees of their technological advancement. In some factories producing semiconductors, they were well along, while in other areas they were still far behind. They are obtaining whatever technology they can from the Japanese, the French, and the Italians, but they prefer to do business with the United States. They made that abundantly clear, partly because they like doing business with the United States but also because they realize that most of the software and program activity is better suited to the English language than it is to the Chinese or Japanese language or some of the other conventional programs that are available.

China represents a vast opportunity for American technology companies, and the United States should not leave the door closed. It will serve the United States' best interests to adopt the administration's new policy, for pursuant to an agreement by the Chinese, the United States will be able to control dual-use or end-use application of that technology.

Finally, there is a need to comment on the legislative status of the Export Administration Act that is presently before Congress. The Senate bill was favorably reported by the Senate Finance Committee after Senators Garn and Heinz reconciled their differences on foreign policy and national security controls. That bill may have some rough going on the Senate floor, but pursuant to the agreement of these two knowledgeable people on the legislation, they might be able to fend off most amendments.

On the House side, there has always been fear because, in the past, whenever the Export Administration Act has come up for renewal, the national security-oriented legislators have been well-organized and effective in adding amendments that have tightened the controls. There has been a noticeable absence of that effort on the House side this year. Some of the change is due to the fact that some of the national security people in the House are no longer serving as representatives. In addition, the Armed Services Committee, which has a vested interest in this issue, set up a task force headed by Congressman Hutto, and they have taken a rather moderate approach to this legislation. The committee will be offering only one amendment--that dealing with militarily critical technology--which is something quite acceptable. So there has not been much opposition to renewal of the act.

Another factor aiding passage of the House bill is that the business community has been much better organized, through the Chamber of Commerce, the National Association of Manufacturers, the Business Roundtable, and various trade associations. If one were to ask any of these groups today to list the number one export problem or issue they face, they would probably say it was the Export Administration Act. They have all lobbied extensively in both the House and the Senate, and they are much better prepared in getting their message across than they have been in the past. The only worry that many have on the foreign policy section is the result of the Korean Air Lines incident. With emotions running high, and this legislation due for consideration of the floor, it could be a bad time for consideration.

Last, there is a new section of the bill concerning trade with South Africa. The provision would ban the importation of Krugerrand gold, implement the Sullivan principles on businesses located in South Africa, and place certain restrictions on bank loans to the government of South Africa for other than educational or institutional purposes.

The only other concern facing those interested in passing the Export Administration Act is that Senator Stevens from Alaska has placed a hold on the Export Administration Act because of another control that he opposes in the bill.  It has nothing to do with national security or foreign policy controls, but is the area of the bill relating to materials in short supply.  This provision provides authority for the President to impose controls, restrictions, or even a ban on the export of a resource or a material that is in scarce supply in the United States.  There is one such control on the export of Western red cedar, another on the export of horses, and this one happens to deal with the export of Alaskan crude oil.  Senator Stevens would like to see that oil go to Japan, a country that has some interest in the matter, so he is attempting to slow down if not halt the movement of that bill to the Senate floor.  That could be a problem because he will make a request to extend Senate consideraton of the legislation for 60 days.

# 15

# THE EXPORT ADMINISTRATION ACT: THE SENATE VIEW

## John Heinz

My experience with the Export Administration Act is relatively short. It comes from almost seven years of having served first as ranking minority member and now as chairman of the International Finance and Monetary Policy subcommittee. To put that in perspective, one witness at Senate hearings earlier this year discussed his more than 30-year association with the act and its predecessors.

That broader perspective can be helpful, since in many respects the act mirrors other changes that have taken place in post-World War II U.S. foreign relations:

1. The advent of the Cold War and U.S. determination to deny critical technology to the Soviets and other Eastern bloc nations.
2. The growth in importance of trade and the internationalization of the U.S. economy.
3. Growing pressure in the United States to increase exports.

In past years, one or another of these considerations was paramount. The 1979 Export Administration Act, for example, is much more an exporter's bill than were earlier versions. That is a tribute to the previous subcommittee chairman, Adlai Stevenson.

Today Congress faces renewal of the act in a period of unprecedented conflict over its basic principles. Every proposal to amend the act is controversial, and renewal promises to be long and difficult.

Yet the need for resolving these conflicts is greater than ever. The U.S. trade deficit for 1983 will top $70 billion, almost double the deficit of 1982. At the same time, the growing budget deficit at home has produced excessively high interest rates and an overvalued dollar.

Martin Feldstein, chairman of the Council of Economic Advisors, may not be the most powerful official in the government, but he has a major advantage over the others--he is right. When he asserts that the dollar's value over the past three years has been inflated nearly 50 percent due to high interest rates, he is laying out the single most important cause of the U.S. trade deficit and demonstrating clearly the link between the domestic economy and the world market. He is also reminding us that only by reducing the budget deficit can the United States reduce interest rates and ultimately its trade deficit.

This overvaluation is apparent if one examines what has happened to the U.S. market share in several key sectors: In 1982, commercial aircraft exports were down 47 percent from their 1981 level; in the first half of 1983, construction machinery exports were off 44 percent and machine tool exports were off 42 percent from the level of the comparable period in 1982. In fact, total exports declined 10 percent over that same period, and that was on top of a 9.2 percent decline in 1982, as compared to 1981.

Before discussing how to solve these problems, it is useful to take a few moments to review how this country got where it is and what it has at stake. Perhaps it would be helpful to review the lessons of the changing economic and political realities of the postwar era.

The first thing we learned as a result of the war was the clear link between economic policy and foreign policy. The Allies won the war in large part because of their stronger and larger economic base, and the United States has been learning ever since that it can project its political power through economic power--positively, through aid and trade, and negatively, through controls and embargoes.

Second, the West's interest in economic weapons has been enhanced by the growing destructiveness of military weapons. With the advent of nuclear warfare, military conflict would likely become the final conflict, and nations have begun to search for measures short of war to show their displeasure or to force another country into better behavior.

Third, the world has witnessed the growth of a true global market. The increased sophistication and speed of transportation and communication permit a new quantity and variety of global trade. Companies that never thought of exporting now do it as a matter of course. Other companies that thought their domestic market position was safe are finding themselves buried by import competition.

Fourth, that world market is more important than ever because of declines in the rate of growth of the U.S. domestic economy. As the economy matures, exports are more important to it because they are the last major growth area.

Finally, we are coming to the realization that these developments do not happily complement each other. If we export more, we increase the risk of transferring critical technology to our adversaries. It is harder to use export controls as weapons because the proexport constituency in this country has broadened. On the other hand, if exports are controlled more, the economy grows less at a time when we need all the economic good news we can get.

Yet at the same time, the country has reached a point where its policymakers are increasingly tempted to use economic weapons--because there is no safe alternative--at the very time when such weapons hurt the most and help the least, thanks to uncooperative allies.

Since the act was last renewed more than four years ago, there have been two major efforts to impose economic sanctions--the Carter grain embargo in the wake of the Soviet invasion of Afghanistan and the Reagan pipeline controls. Neither achieved its political objectives and both caused considerable economic damage. In agriculture, the United States lost market share that it will never recapture. In industry, U.S. businesses lost their reputation as credible, reliable suppliers, and, as politicians should know better than anyone, credibility is the hardest quality to restore.

Despite the apparent failure of previous trade sanctions, earlier this month people were seriously suggesting that this country take the same actions in response to the shooting down of the Korean Air Lines 747. The President wisely chose not to take those steps, but that controversy shows the conflicts that remain.

What are those conflicts that have come to a head, and how should a responsible and responsive Export Administration Act address them? First, there is a conflict between the right to export and the need to restrict exports for national security purposes. Second, there is a conflict between the need to establish U.S. exporters as reliable, credible suppliers and the pressures to make political statements with economic weapons.

These pressures are sometimes from the right--to impose restrictions on communist regimes--but they are equally often from the center and the left--to demonstrate U.S. disapproval of racism, terrorism, and human rights violations. The reasoning is simple. Obviously the United States is not going to declare war and invade Iraq because that country supports terrorism, but how does this country show its displeasure? The United States refuses to sell them commercial aircraft, among other things. That sends a message--and makes us (except for Boeing) feel better-- although it probably does not make much difference to the Iraqis, who simply buy from Airbus.

Saying that is not meant to belittle the policy. Terrorism is evil. Everyone deplores it and wants the government to fight it in every possible way. Everyone wants to show disapproval. That is what makes these conflicts so difficult--both sides have a point. Of course the United States should export, but we should not let the Soviets build their war machine with our equipment. Of course U.S. businesses should be reliable exporters, but as the leader of the free world, the United States should stand up for its principles and demonstrate its disapproval of unacceptable behavior.

Right now, the House, the Senate, and the administration are all wrestling with these conflicts. Each has produced a bill, and each deserves some comment. The administration bill represents a failure to confront these issues and thus postpones dealing with the serious problem of the deficit. All the conflicting views just described are well-represented in the federal buraucracy. The Defense Department, by and large, is sympathetic to exporters. The State Department seems most concerned about how other

nations will react to controls, and the Treasury Department
cares about the role of the Customs Service.

These differences are not new or unusual; neither is
the failure to reconcile them. The administration bill
represents a least-common-denominator approach. It includes
only minor issues agreeable to all parties, and it avoids
the major issues. The bill does not deal with how to improve allied discipline on controls. It does not deal with
the foreign availability question, a critical element in the
effectiveness of any controls. It ignores exporters' concerns about loosening controls on exports to Western nations
and on providing contract sanctity, and it does not deal
with the serious questions that have been raised about enforcement. In other words, it cops out. The White House
has not yet forced agreement on the tough issues, though
that may still happen. Until it does there will be no truly
effective administration presence on the Export Administration Act.

The House Foreign Affairs Committee, to its credit,
has grappled seriously with the basic conflicts. Unfortunately, the House bill is flawed because it tilts toward exporters to the point of ignoring national security concerns.
For example, the House bill removes validated license requirements for all exports to COCOM nations, regardless of
their militarily critical nature. This ignores the mixed
effort U.S. allies have made in preventing diversion to the
East, and it eliminates any possibility of maintaining a
paper trail to trace and stop such diversion.

The House bill provides for putting an item on general
license if all applications for a validated license have
been approved in the preceding year. The typical bureau-
crat's response to this provision will be denials on the
last day of the year in order to preserve the bureaucracy's
options.

Finally, in sharp contrast to its sacrifice of national security interests, the House bill surprisingly deals
exporters a severe blow on their most important issue--the
sanctity of contracts. Liberals concerned about taking
strong stands against human rights violations and conserva-
tives wanting maximum flexibility for anti-Soviet retalia-
tion teamed up to provide explicit authority to break contracts in a wide variety of circumstances.

These are not the only provisions of the House bill, but they demonstrate an unacceptable tilt against national security interests and against exporters in the vital area of contract sanctity.

The Senate bill represents a more balanced compromise, in part because of the different process that developed it. The Senate effort began in February 1983 when Senator Garn, the Banking Committee chairman, and I introduced sharply different bills. His would create an independent Office of Strategic Trade to handle licensing and enforcement and was admittedly designed to tighten the process. My bill, in contrast, was more clearly reflective of the interests of exporters.

Ultimately a compromise between these two bills was worked out, partly because everyone wanted to avoid a prolonged and bitter battle and partly because nobody was sure of winning a confrontation. Instead, by working together, the Senate has produced a stronger, better balanced bill with respect to both national security and foreign policy controls.

In the national security area, the Senate bill is designed to achieve five specific objectives. First, it works to increase multilateral discipline and cooperation. In addition to seeking to upgrade COCOM to treaty status, thereby giving it more credibility, the Senate bill gives the President discretionary authority to deny the right to import to companies that violate either U.S. export control laws or COCOM standards. This provision is essential to convince U.S. allies that Washington is serious about an effective control process and determined to enforce it aggressively.

The bill also attempts to simplify and reduce the licensing burden, particularly for high-technology end-products going to U.S. allies. It creates a Comprehensive Operations License, which will permit multiple exports of technology and related goods to an affiliate abroad if satisfactory controls and safeguards are in place. In addition, the bill provides for general license exports of most items to COCOM nations. It also reduces licensing times by one-third.

Third, the bill gives the issue of foreign availability a determining role in licensing decisions. It makes no sense for the United States to prohibit an export if it is available elsewhere.

Fourth, the Senate legislation seeks to clarify the murky relationship between the Defense Department and the Commerce Department in license review by providing for the Defense Department's right to review applications, subject to Commerce concurrence, when there is a clear risk of diversion of militarily critical items. This provision has been the subject of some misinterpretation in the business community. In fact, it is an accurate representation of the way the 1979 act was supposed to operate, and it makes it clear that a Defense Department review would occur only with Commerce Department approval.

Finally, the bill upgrades the management of the licensing process and improves enforcement. To correct existing deficiencies, the Senate bill transfers enforcement responsibility to the Customs Service, an agency with more resources and more experience in enforcement than the Commerce Department.

Taken together, these changes provide the necessary balance between the rights of exporters and the national security concerns of the United States. In the area of foreign policy controls, the Senate bill focuses on the lost credibility of U.S. exporters, seeking to restore that credibility without inhibiting the U.S. ability to use export controls for statements of principle. The Senate bill addresses the credibility question in three ways.

First, it requires more thorough consideration of a higher standard before controls are imposed. In past cases the required consultation with Congress had become little more than consultation a few hours in advance of a presidential action. Consideration of the statutory criteria for imposing controls has become pro forma. By changing these criteria to determinations that must be made and submitted to Congress in advance, the bill makes the decision-making process more serious and more consensual without tying the President's hands.

Second, it addresses the credibility issue by protecting existing supply relationships through contract sanctity. This is the core of the Senate bill. By making export controls prospective, the legislation simultaneously restores

U.S. exporters' credibility and responds to allied complaints about the extraterritorial application of U.S. law.

At the same time, the President retains authority to impose more severe measures, including those that break contracts, under the International Emergency Economic Powers Act; the Senate bill amends that law to make this clear. The Senate bill follows this route because of the sponsors' belief that if the imposition of controls is so important as to require the breaking of contracts, with all the damage that causes the economy, then it is important enough to warrant the declaration of an emergency.

Third, the bill addresses the credibility issue by giving foreign availability a determining role in issuing licenses for items subject to foreign policy controls. As in the case of national security controls, it is useless to impose controls when comparable products are available from other sources. The key is to obtain multilateral cooperation in the control program. The Senate bill encourages such cooperation by making foreign availability a more significant factor in approving a license six months after controls are imposed. That will provide time for consultation with the allies on an effective control program. At the same time, it will give the President sufficient flexibility, even after the initial six-month period, to impose controls in cases where circumstances warrant.

These provisions are by no means the only ones in the bill. All told, there are over 80 amendments to current law in the Senate bill. They do present, however, a fair compromise. Senator Garn and I have frequently found ourselves caught between those who would export nothing for fear of critical technology falling into Soviet hands and those who would sell everything regardless of that risk. We have listened patiently to those who acknowledge the need for exporter credibility but always have one or two special cases that are somehow more important. We have contended with those who want to tilt the Export Administration Act to suit their own short-term purposes. Thus far we have been successful in defending our compromise package from attack. Taken as a whole, the Senate bill serves our national security purposes. It protects the economic interests of our business executives and our farmers. Most important, it preserves the integrity of the act.

# 16

# HIGH TECHNOLOGY AND THE EXPORT ADMINISTRATION ACT

## Paul Freedenberg

Nine months ago, when this author was asked to write an analysis of what was likely to happen with the debate over the Export Administration Act, the article concluded with the following statement:

> The debate over the renewal of the Export Ad-
> ministration Act is certain to be a major leg-
> islative battle. Many of the critical questions
> of trade and foreign policy and national secu-
> rity which have proven to be so difficult to
> solve over the last few years will be high-
> lighted in the Act renewal. Our nation's
> ability to protect its technological lead over
> its potential adversaries, the strength and
> economic viability of some of our most pro-
> ductive and innovative high technology com-
> panies, and the question of our President's
> prerogatives and ability to pursue foreign
> policy and national security goals all will
> come together as part of the debate over the
> Act's renewal. The fact that the Export Admin-
> istration Act of 1983 will have a profound
> effect on our nation's security and economic
> well-being in the balance of the decade prom-
> ises to make the debate lively and contentious
> and the final product impossible to predict.

169

That was nine months ago, but the debate so far over that act has proven that prediction to be quite accurate. Currently, we are in the final weeks of fiscal year 1983, and the act will expire in nine days. It has yet to get to either the Senate or the House floor. Many things have acted to impede its progress. Committees in both houses finished considering the bill in June, but in late July, when the act was due to come up in the Senate, the Finance Committee raised objections to the import control sanctions provided for in the act. The import control controversy has delayed consideration of the entire bill, and since it is such a hot topic of debate and such an important issue and directly ties into the comments of Joseph E. Pattison regarding extraterritoriality, this chapter will devote a good amount of time to the subject.

The other factor that has entered into the debate to impede the bill's progress is that the act has three parts. The act gives the President power to control exports for purposes of national security. It also provides control authority for foreign policy purposes, which was the justification used in the pipeline decision. Finally, it provides control authority for items in short supply. The short-supply section, the bill's managers were hoping, would be a nonissue this time around, but it has proven to be the impediment to consideration on the Senate floor because it includes a provision that makes it virtually impossible to export Alaskan oil. That provision, although strongly supported by a number of Senators and by a majority of the House, has caused the Senators from Alaska to block consideration of the act, hoping somehow to get leverage as the act is stalled and thereby obtain bargaining on the short-supply issue. As a result, one can assume that the debate will come down to the final hours of fiscal year 1983.

The continuing resolution, which provides authority for agencies that have not yet received appropriations, will probably be the vehicle with which Congress will extend the act for a short period. It is doubtful that any senators who are major figures on this subject, or administration decisionmakers, have yet decided what to do. We could get down to quite a cliffhanger on this issue, and it would be difficult to predict the outcome because one gets down to the question of whether any particular issue, such as

Alaskan oil, or any particular provision is important
enough to have the President's power to control exports
expire. His power to control exports expired once before,
but at that time the Trading with the Enemy Act granted the
President such broad authority that he was able to use it as
a substitute for the Export Administration Act to provide
authority for the control of exports. Revisions in 1977 of
the Trading with the Enemy Act have taken some of that power
away from the President, so it is not clear that there is
legislative power for the President to control exports other
than that contained in the Export Administration Act.

The reason why it is such a tough battle, besides the
Alaskan oil issue, is that the Export Administration Act
Amendments of 1983 and the act itself can be best explained
by looking at the inherent tension between the desire to
curtail the transfer of militarily critical high technology
to the Soviet Union and the belief tht the United States is
in danger of losing its traditional export markets for high
technology. In simplified terms, one might describe it as
the tension between the military and the commercial challenges for the United States in the 1980s and beyond--the
question of which threat is more significant, that posed by
the Soviet Union or that posed by Japan.

Since this chapter focuses on high-technology trade
with the Eastern bloc, it will look at the Senate's efforts
to modify the rules of that trading relationship. The Banking Committee worked from two premises. The first premise,
which was never stated but was an important part of the
thinking, is that Yuri Andropov, who was the director of
the KGB effort to acquire Western technology for Soviet industry and for their military effort for the past 15 years,
can be expected, as the leader of the Soviet Union, to keep
this effort as a top priority. This is particularly likely
since this effort is the only way that there can be any hope
of a quick fix to the sort of technological inferiority
demonstrated in the 1982 Bekaa Valley battles between the
U.S.-backed Israelis and the Soviet-backed Syrians.

Those who remember that air battle during the Israeli
incursion into Lebanon will remember that there were reports
of many Soviet military delegations coming to look at what
happened to the air defenses and to the Soviet aircraft during the Syrian battles with the Israelis; they were trying to

judge the significance of the defeats. This could very well
be seen as a watershed event for the Soviet military thinking. One can never tell until history unfolds, but just as
in the memoirs of Khrushchev, where one sees that there was
a great humiliation during the Cuban Missile Crisis, for
many Soviets there was a similar feeling of humiliation
following their defeats in the Bekaa Valley. Those defeats
clearly will have an effect on their future military planning and on the priority they place on modernization and on
acquisition of Western technology.

It is also true, however, that there are few technologies in which the United States still possesses a monopoly. This fact was the second premise from which the
Senate Banking Committee was operating. Any effective controls require Western cooperation. Unilateral or counter-
productive controls on technology are likely to penalize
U.S. exporters while failing to deny that very technology
to the Soviet Union. Moreover, such controls are likely to
erode further U.S. shares of vital markets and to deny the
profits necessary to continue commercial research and development. The Pentagon realizes quite readily that much
of the high-technology weaponry on which the American military depends has a spin-off effect from commercial research
and development. It is no longer as much a dependence of
commercial technology on military research and development
as it is a dependence of military weaponry on commercial
research and development. U.S. technological superiority,
in turn, depends on continued U.S. market share of vital
export markets. If one looks at U.S. high-technology companies, one can see that almost all are very heavily dependent on export markets.

The Senate bill tried to respond to both of those concerns. It tightened enforcement through the transfer of
enforcement authority from the Commerce Department to the
Customs Service, and it provided new enforcement powers to
the U.S. government. This transfer was based on hearings,
conducted largely under Senator Sam Nunn's supervision, held
in May 1982 by the Permanent Investigation subcommittee of
the Government Affairs Committee. The subcommittee concluded that there were great gaps in the enforcement capabilities of the Commerce Department. (There is no need to
go into the details.)

The Commerce Department has responded positively to the revelations of that subcommittee and to its own Inspector General's analysis of the gaps in export enforcement capability. Despite this change, there was still a feeling in the Senate Banking Committee that, while that response is certainly welcome and overdue, one cannot be confident that the same level of intensity with regard to enforcement can be guaranteed for the future. We are not always going to have Lionel Olmer and Larry Brady and the other people over at the Commerce Department who have responded so well during the last year. So there was a consensus that the enforcement ought to be transferred to an agency with a tradition of tough law enforcement. That is, in large part, the origin of that provision.

There is another major provision in the Senate bill that is quite controversial in the business community, and that is an amendment to section 10g that gives the Defense Department the right to review West-West licenses. The feeling of the committee was that this amendment clarified the 1979 act and that there would be guarantees built into it so that there would not be a grinding to a halt of the export licensing process through delay and excessive caution on the part of the Defense Department. The amendment requires consultation between the Department of Commerce and the Department of Defense and, most important, calls for a case to be made that there is a clear risk of diversion before such review would take place.

There is also a mandate for an upgrading of COCOM. (COCOM is the multilateral control organization consisting of the NATO allies, plus Japan, and minus Iceland. It is of an informal nature.) One of the provisions in the Senate bill would call on the President to negotiate an increase in that organization to treaty status. There are also a number of other provisions that would upgrade the list construction and enforcement procedures within COCOM. Again, the feeling is that it is foolish for the United States to try to enforce export controls unilaterally. Unless one has an effective multilateral organization, there is no way this effort can succeed.

The balance of this chapter will focus on another important and controversial provision of the Senate bill. The bill provides for national security import sanctions for companies that violate either U.S. national security or COCOM regulations. The reasoning behind this provision is that the first objective of the U.S. export control system is to prevent the illegal export of controlled goods and technology. The second goal is, in the event of the illegal export, to provide sufficiently effective penalties to deter any future violations. The committee felt that this deterrent would be greatly enhanced by providing the President with the authority to deny violators the privilege of importing items into the United States.

Clearly this is a very powerful sanction, and just as clearly, if a company had to choose between engaging in illicit trade with our potential adversaries or having access to the U.S. market, it would not be very difficult for it to make the decision. It would choose the U.S. market. The committee did not believe that the United States had any obligation to keep its markets open to those who could be proven to have endangered U.S. national security, and there was evidence presented to the committee, in both open and closed sessions, that allied cooperation has not always been at the level of effectiveness necessary to maintain U.S. national security.

There were cases presented in which items that clearly were on the U.S. control list and on the COCOM list had been licensed to Eastern Europe. The proof was that the items showed up at trade shows with Eastern European manufacturers who had obtained the licenses—in one case from Japan. There has been another case where U.S. equipment that had a dual use—not only air control capability but air defense capability, which greatly enhanced Soviet capacity to track and intercept U.S. aircraft—was resold very knowingly by a neutral-country company to the Soviet Union. That particular company had a multibillion dollar market in the United States, whereas this sale might have been worth a few tens of millions of dollars. There was no authority for the U.S. government to provide any sanction, even though it was very clear that the company knew what it was doing and very knowingly violated a U.S. reexport provision that was in the license.

There was another case in which a company in an allied Western European nation exported highly sophisticated switching equipment of a level of telecommunication sophis-

tication higher than that used by NATO.  U.S. attempts to
get that equipment export blocked or delayed in shipment
were futile, despite the fact that the company's actions
violated the COCOM arrangement.

The committee felt there were a number of provisions
in the bill that would put a greater dependence on COCOM
and on allied cooperation for enforcement of reexport.  In
the absence of some sanction, some confidence that technology that was now being controlled by U.S. allies could
be effectively controlled and that the United States would
have some ultimate say in its reexport, the committee could
not in good conscience vote for increased flexibility in
licensing provisions.  For example, the committee increased
the use of multiple licensing, through the use of what is
known as a comprehensive operations license--which would
allow companies to have multiple shipments of like products
to approved consignees.  But the committee built into the
process the national security import sanction as well.  In
doing so, it went beyond the administration's request.

The administration had only allowed in its proposed
bill for import sanctions for the violation of U.S. export
control laws, not for violation of the COCOM list and regulations drawn up subject to that list.  The explanation
for this was that if a case were to occur where the United
States felt that one of its allies, or a neutral country,
was not enforcing its own laws--all of these countries have
laws against the reexport of such militarily sensitive
technology--then U.S. officials would very quietly consult
with the ally and try to explain the problem. The U.S. reaction should not become an international incident, and the
ally should not first find out about it in the New York
Times.  The committee felt strongly, however, that import
sanctions were necessary in these cases.

The bill produced by the committee, which will soon
be going to the Senate floor, is one in which an important
balance was struck.  U.S. exporters can be assured that the
system will be more efficient and more responsive to their
needs.  At the same time, those concerned about national
security will have the confidence that there will be vigor-
ous enforcement, appropriate penalties, and an end to the
institutional bias in favor of exports that has marked the
U.S. export control process in the past.  Shortened time

frames for review and approval of export licensing and the increased use of multiple licenses should ensure that U.S. exporters will not lose sales as a result of unnecessary delay or bureaucratic inefficiency. Just as important, however, Defense Department review of West-West licenses and import sanctions against those who violate U.S. reexport control regulations or COCOM regulations should prove to be an effective offset to proexport biases in the system and a reassurance to those who fear that increased efficiency will also increase the probability of Western technology hemorrhage to the East.

# 17

# IMPROVING FOREIGN POLICY TRADE CONTROLS

## Raymond J. Waldmann

This chapter analyzes the power of the President to control exports for foreign policy purposes and examines some current proposals to limit that power. Under present law, the President may impose foreign policy controls in accordance with the terms of the Export Administration Act of 1979, as amended by the Export Administration Act of 1981. This act, however, expires on September 30, 1983, and its renewal is a subject of intense interest.

Foreign policy export controls are broadly defined in the Export Administration Act (hereafter the act) as those imposed on the export of goods and technology "where necessary to further significantly the foreign policy of the United States or to fulfill its declared international obligations," to secure the removal of foreign country restrictions on access to supplies, and to encourage other countries to combat terrorism.[1]

The Export Administration Act also provides for several other types of export controls. National security controls can be imposed to restrict the export of goods and technology that "would make a significant contribution to

AUTHOR'S NOTE: Excerpted from a book to be published by the Center for Law and National Security, University of Virginia, Charlottesville.

the military potential of any other country or combination of countries which would prove detrimental to the national security of the United States." Those imposed "to restrict the export of goods where necessary to protect the domestic economy from the excessive drain of scarce materials and to reduce the serious inflationary impact of foreign demand" are called short-supply controls. The act provides that, in most instances, medicines and medical equipment cannot be controlled, and the "Fenwick Amendment" imposes conditions on the control of food exports. One important provision of the act exempts it from judicial review; other sections deal with foreign boycotts, procedures for processing export license applications, provisions for relief in hardship cases, definitions of violations, enforcement, reporting to Congress, and miscellaneous provisions.

The congressional findings and basic declaration of U.S. export control policy contain an idealized and inherently contradictory set of policies. On the one hand, the act states that trade with all countries enjoying diplomatic relations with the United States should be encouraged and the uncertainties of controls should be minimized. On the other hand, it explicitly recognizes the necessity of controlling exports for reasons of national security, foreign policy, and short supply.

The act encourages the United States to apply controls in concert with its allies and in accordance with international agreements, but at the same time, it grants the President full authority to impose controls unilaterally. The act requires the Secretary of Commerce, in carrying out the provisions of the act, to keep the public fully apprised of changes in control policy and procedures and to meet regularly with business executives to obtain their views, but it also allows the Secretary to impose controls without prior notice or consultation with either Congress or the public. Furthermore, the imposition of controls is not subject to judicial review.

The act and the administration of export controls, particularly those imposed for foreign policy reasons, have become a focal point for debate. Temperatures rise when the act is up for renewal, and this time the debate is even more intense because of controls imposed following the invasion of Afghanistan and, more recently, the Polish military takeover. In both cases, the business community bore the brunt of the cost and complained bitterly.


THE PRESENT ACT

The 1979 act emphasized exports and attempted to confine controls to those areas where their use was deemed to be "essential."[2] For the first time, it explicitly separated foreign policy controls from national security controls, making the basis for applying each type different and explicit. While the authorities and procedures remained unchanged, the policy statements in the act and in the legislative history tilted the act toward exports and away from controls. By stating that exports should only be controlled when necessary to further fundamental national security, foreign policy, or short-supply objectives, the 1979 act attempted to provide a stricter test. This hortatory language was not integrated with the substantive provisions of the act and thus has had little practical effect since 1979.

This act also limited presidential discretion and authority to control exports. Bills in both houses of Congress proposed even stricter limits, but the Carter administration opposed the most restrictive bills as hindering executive power to conduct foreign affairs. Nevertheless, the 1979 act incorporated for the first time some substantive provisions to limit executive discretion. These included:

1. a list of decision factors that must be considered before foreign policy controls can be imposed:
   a. probability of success,
   b. compatibility with overall foreign policy,
   c. reactions of third countries,
   d. effect on U.S. export performance and the exports of companies,
   e. enforceability, and
   f. the consequences of not imposing the controls;
2. a requirement that the Secretary of Commerce consult with appropriate U.S. industries and that the President consult with Congress in every possible instance before

imposing controls, and that an annual report be sent to
Congress detailing, among other things, the effectiveness of any foreign policy controls;

3.  a requirement that all foreign policy controls expire
    one year after imposition unless explicitly extended
    by the President.

These additional requirements have imposed some administrative burdens, but it is clear that they do not
limit executive discretion. Instead, they provide a set of
procedures to regulate the imposition of controls and, if
anything, make the imposition of controls more rather than
less likely.

One reason for dissatisfaction with the current law
is the absence of any outside review by either courts or
Congress, for the act contains a provision in Section 13
explicitly exempting decisions made under the act from judicial review. Section 13 provides that the functions exercised under the act are excluded from the operation of sections of Title 5 of the U.S. Code, the Administrative Procedures Act. In fact, the only portion of the act subject
to judicial review is Section 11(c)(2), which covers the
imposition of the administrative sanction of suspending or
revoking export authority.

This exemption from judicial review was incorporated
in the 1969 act and continued in all subsequent revisions.
As a result, decisions dealing with the act, and in particular with Section 6 authorizing foreign policy controls,
are scarce. In one of the few judicial comments on the act,
the court, in U.S. v. Brumage, stated that the section regu-
lating foreign commerce is closely related to foreign affairs and national security and is therefore entitled to the
highest presumption of validity.[3] It further found that the
act's provisions controlling exports "for the benefit of
any communist-dominated nation" were not unconstitutionally
vague, even though reasonable people could differ as to the
application of these words.

The most recent test of the authorities granted under
the act came as a result of President Reagan's imposition
of sanctions against the Soviet Union after the declaration
of martial law in Poland. After the extension of controls on
June 22, 1982, to cover exports of foreign-origin goods and

technical data by U.S.-owned or controlled companies abroad and of foreign-produced products of U.S. technical data not previously subject to controls, two of the affected companies, Dresser-France, S.S. and Creusot-Loire, S.A., challenged the U.S. action in court.[4] The District Court for the District of Columbia dismissed the challenge, finding that the Executive Branch was within its authority in imposing the controls and arguing that the plaintiffs had not yet exhausted administrative remedies.

## ASSESSING THE PROPOSALS TO LIMIT EXECUTIVE DISCRETION

Proposals to amend the foreign policy controls of the Export Administration Act fall into two broad categories: those designed to limit the discretion and the authority of the Executive Branch in the imposition of controls and those designed to improve the use of, or limit the damage resulting from, the controls once imposed.

### Repeal the General Delegation to the President

One proposal would require every imposition of controls to be authorized separately and specifically by statute passed by Congress. This proposal is the most radical and the least likely to succeed of the various proposals. It recognizes the need for foreign policy controls yet makes the imposition of them so unlikely that it could be called a de facto renunciation by the U.S. government of its power to impose controls for any reason. Given the pace of congressional action, the absence of congressional leadership on control issues and decisions, the openness of the congressional processes, and the demonstrated success of interest groups in thwarting any congressional action with which they disagree, it would be extremely unlikely that controls would ever be imposed.

Assuming that the President were still interested in proposing controls, they would lose much of their force because of the delays and weakening inevitable in the congressional process. Every congressional debate would pit the President--usually favoring controls--against the business community--opposed to any controls except in the most obvious and egregious cases. This political polarization would hinder attempts to achieve the bipartisan foreign policy or an international consensus so necessary to effective implementation of the controls with allied nations.

While the open congressional process is laudable and indispensable to the U.S. system, the Constitution also provides for a less contentious exercise of power. Negotiations with offending nations to remove objectionable policies often must be conducted in secrecy, or at least out of the limelight. It is therefore the threat of imposing controls, more than their imposition, that can be most useful in achieving a reversal of objectionable policies. Since an offending country must be presumed to understand the difficulties the administration would encounter in seeking congressional imposition of controls, the threat of sanctions would become an empty one. Certainly any debate in Congress about the wisdom, necessity, and domestic cost of controls would weaken the U.S. negotiating position.

Finally, it should be recognized that the controls imposed now are often modified in application by the executive, since to impose controls explicitly by statutory language would make their administration almost unacceptably rigid. If Congress had to authorize every imposition of controls, special conditions and even exceptions could be written into legislation, reducing the impact of controls. Provisions imposing time limits, specifying expected results and procedural steps, and stating necessary conditions for controls would all find their way into the statute, making the administration of the act virtually impossible. These limits would perhaps achieve the unstated objective of those proposing repeal of the delegation: the total elimination of foreign policy controls.

Involve Congress More Directly

These proposals would amend the act to involve Congress more explicitly in the process of imposing controls by allowing congressional disapproval by concurrent resolution, by requiring reports to Congress before and after the

imposition of controls, and by allowing a public review of
the controls.

While many of the objections to repeal of the delegation apply here as well, they are muted in force because the
President would still be in a position to take action with
only a congressional "veto" to fight. In essence, the possibility of congressional expression already exists in the
form of a resolution against any controls with which it dis-
agrees. In any case, the effect of any "veto" would be moot
now under the Supreme Court ruling declaring the one-house
veto unconstitutional. The novel element in this proposal
would be the possibility of effective reversal of the executive action.

It must be recognized that, in practice, consultation
with the congressional leadership in advance of controls is
designed to secure congressional support if not outright approval; thus consultation will occur whether mandated or not.
If Congress appears likely to overturn the controls, then
that prediction must be taken into account, but it may not
be dispositive. In other words, the President might impose
controls to achieve negotiating objectives, to strengthen
allied resolve, to react to a particular crisis, or for some
other reason, knowing full well that in time Congress would
"veto" the imposition.

The congressional "veto" might have the same consequences for foreign policy and allied cooperation as the repeal of presidential authority to impose controls. The controls could nevertheless have some effect for the period of
time imposed as a demonstration of the administration's will;
this could be, regardless of the evident split in U.S. policy, an important byproduct of a full-scale congressional
reversal. The pressures of domestic interest would be brought
to bear on Congress and would polarize decision making along
political or interest group lines. On balance, therefore,
the gains in openness of the process are outweighed by the
costs to foreign policy.

The other conditions imposed under this proposal—requiring reports to Congress and public review of proposed
controls—have little purpose when standing alone except to
force more public discussion of controls without affecting
the decision to impose the controls. The necessity to report, one could argue, enforces needed discipline and thus

directs the administrators to a better decision. On the other hand, the mere reporting requirements have little effect without tighter substantive requirements. There are already too many "reports" required of the executive that do nothing except keep writers and filers busy. In fact, the process often degenerates into a game of determining whether the filed report was adequate rather than discussing its contents. Such formalism should have no place in the revision of the act.

## Tighten the Constraints

Proponents of tightened constraints would amend the act to require the President to perform certain procedural and analytical tasks before imposing controls. This is the most reasonable group of proposals with which to carry out the intent of Congress; that intent is to allow the imposition of controls and, at the same time, to circumscribe their use. The current act specifies a number of "decision factors" that the President should take into account. By imposing certain procedural steps and analytical checkpoints on the executive, Congress would reinforce its intent that these factors be considered, though it would not rejudge or review the President's decisions.

The major problem with this approach is the danger that it would turn export control decisions into the foreign policy equivalent of environmental impact statements. One of the consequences of requiring impact statements for federally funded projects has been an enormous complication, delay, and judicialization of decision making; any opponent can bring the matter to court at almost any stage to question the scope, timeliness, adequacy, completeness, and even results of the impact statement. Therefore, one could foresee, perhaps even presume, similar legalistic arguments being raised against an export control decision by those most affected, the U.S. exporters.

Regardless of the decisions made, the possibility that a court, a congressional committee, or even some public review panel might scrutinize and inevitably second-guess export control decisions must give one pause. Even if the review were limited to procedural compliance with the act, substantive foreign policy questions would be raised, given the nature of the decision factors supposedly to be taken into account. How would a court, for example, review the adequacy of allied consultation unless it had complete knowledge of all the negotiations and discussions leading up to the imposition of controls--matters traditionally and quite properly left to the Executive Branch? Judicial or congressional review of such matters would arguably be declared unconstitutional.

The fundamental conclusion, it is becoming clear, is that the basic structure of the exercise of foreign policy controls through Executive Branch action is sound and should persist through the renewal of the act. Improvements can be made in the implementation of controls, however, and these will be discussed in the next section. While some improvements would further limit executive discretion, they would not challenge the basic authority of the President alone to impose foreign policy controls unless he did not follow the guidelines of the act.

## ASSESSING PROPOSALS TO IMPROVE CONTROLS

### Sanctity of Contract

This provision has been suggested by several business groups, is contained in the administration's bill, and is likely to survive in the congressional renewal. It softens the impact of controls by limiting their effect to future transactions, thereby allowing existing contracts to be fulfilled. This provision would achieve the major business goal of making controls more predictable in application, and it would put manufactured exports on the same footing as agricultural exports, which already enjoy such protection.

The major disadvantage of this provision is that it substantially weakens export controls. It gives the target nation the breathing room (270 days for delivery of previously contracted goods is the administration's proposal) to find alternative sources of supply or to develop substitutes, and it provides a nine-month hiatus or "phony war" before the controls bite. This will quite correctly be perceived by target nations and allies alike as a half-hearted imposi-

tion of controls, calling into question the convictions behind the decision itself.


## Extraterritorial Application

Certain U.S. companies involved in the Yamal gas pipeline were placed in an impossible position when, after other
countries refused to support the sanctions against the Soviet
Union, they were subjected to directly conflicting governmental decrees. As a result, pressure has built for some
limitation on extraterritorial application of export controls. Currently, export controls are imposed on persons
within the U.S. jurisdiction regardless of citizenship or
location. Some see this as undue reach of U.S. laws, and it
is likely that some limitation will be enacted. The need is
to limit realistically the exercise of executive authority
to those cases that can be defended, not only politically
but legally, and to smooth relations with the allies.

Congress already has accepted, in the 1979 act (as
well as in the International Economic Emergency Powers Act),
the need for reaching out to U.S. and foreign companies that
might violate controls through foreign subsidiaries, foreign
production and licensees, reexport, or other devices. Rather
than instituting a total ban on extraterritorial application,
it would be better to specify in legislation those cases beyond U.S. jurisdiction. These could include, for example,
cases in which U.S. jurisdiction could not be sustained under
U.S. or international law, cases where the U.S. contacts are
limited, cases where no U.S. origin goods or technology are
involved, or cases where the foreign government decree is
not in violation of an agreement with the United States.
These are the cases for which extraterritorial application
of U.S. controls causes the greatest harm, and they should
be dealt with explicitly, leaving open other cases where extraterritorial applications may be necessary and proper.


## Required Cooperation

It is difficult to justify imposing costs on the U.S.
economy to achieve allied ends when the costs are not shared

by the allies.  Controls on U.S. exports violate basic norms
of fairness if other nations do not impose similar controls
(although the problem of extraterritorial jurisdiction dis-
appears if the potential suppliers also deny their exporters
the market of the target country).  The aim of this proposal
is to level the playing field, at least among the major players, by requiring multilateral controls.

There are, however, significant problems in applying
this proposal that make it almost unworkable.  How many countries must be part of the agreement before the United States
can impose controls?  What if the number falls short?  Are
our hands tied?  Which countries should be included--present
suppliers, potential suppliers, others who sympathize but
are not suppliers?  What would the United States have to pay
in order to secure the agreement of reluctant allies?  Would
these costs be worth it?

Beyond these practical problems lies a conceptual difficulty, for there may well be cases in which the United
States would apply controls knowing they might be undermined
by others.  The United States may feel strongly about an issue such as human rights or terrorism and wish to make a symbolic statement backed by controls, realizing that the chances
of getting agreement are greater if Washington takes the
first step, rather than waiting for others to decide.  The
United States should not deny itself the freedom to take
such steps and should not bind itself in advance to an unworkable condition.  In many cases, it should and will develop a consensus, but in others it may need to act alone.


Meaningful Consultations

Consultations with industry and Congress that share information from all sides are useful because government administrators can explain the basis for the controls and the affected business public can obtain useful information about
the foreign availability of alternatives, the state of the
art in the target country and its options, and the cost to
the U.S. economy of the controls.  In addition, Congress may
have useful information about the political fallout from the
controls and insight into the reaction of the target country
and our allies.

If such information is not shared, consultations will
serve no useful purpose and could degenerate into a formal
"hurdle" to be crossed.  No amount of specificity in the act
about the consultation subjects, timing, scope, and groups
will change this basic fact, and the drafters should not try
to change human nature.  Meaningful consultation will take
place when and only when the administrators believe that
something meaningful will occur.


Time Limits

One proposal to increase the predictability of controls is to shorten the time they can be in effect.  Renewal
would require the same procedures as initial imposition. The
costs of the controls would then be limited to a shorter
period of time, after which business could resume.
This proposal, however, suffers from some problems.
There would be damage to commercial relationships regardless
of the length of time controls operate, for either a six-
month or a one-year hiatus can cause the buyer to consider
the supplier unreliable.  It is a fallacy to assume that a
shorter time limit on controls would be meaningful, for if
the need for controls persists, then they will be renewed;
if not, they should and would be removed as soon as possible,
regardless of the limit specified.


Right to Appeal

The problem raised in the pipeline case by the U.S.
exporter revolved around the timeliness of judicial intervention in the case.  The court found that the petitioner's
rights to due process were not violated by the imposition of
penalties prior to judicial review of the administrative procedures and decisions.  It seems logical to allow the administrative processes to work, especially in sensitive areas
of foreign policy, before a court intervenes.  This is what
Congress intended in exempting the controllers from the Administrative Procedures Act.
To allow earlier judicial review would not only delay
the administration in an area where timing is important but

also interfere with ongoing investigations directly affecting the case to be made against the exporter. Has a violation occurred? How serious is it? Does it undermine the purpose of the controls? These and other questions must be answered before a case is brought to court. To allow judicial review at an earlier stage would be akin to allowing access in a criminal case to the investigating detective's notes and files even before an indictment is brought. The degree of intrusion would probably exceed constitutional limits, thus making it both bad policy and bad law.

Compensation

The desire to compensate companies barred from selling overseas stems from the obvious direct cost to the exporter who has lost sales, but of course the exporter is not alone. Jobs in the exporting company may be affected or lost and many others--including stockholders, lenders, suppliers, carriers, brokers, agents overseas, unions, and even communities--could be affected. Are all or any of these to be compensated, too? If so, how? By the company? Who oversees process? What claims can be considered?

Because of the undesirable precedent and these very real problems, the notion of compensation has not been strongly pushed in the renewal process. It is not likely to be incorporated in the act.

CONCLUSION

The basic structure of the Export Administration Act is sound. The distinctions drawn in 1979 between national security controls and foreign policy controls have clarified the thinking between two quite different types of controls serving different purposes. Both have received congressional support for several decades. Given the unacceptable alternatives of using force to implement foreign policy or lapsing into total inactivity, it is unlikely that Congress will now weaken its support for these controls.

The use of foreign policy controls under the explicit guidelines of the 1979 act is, however, still new. There are ways in which their imposition can be improved by securing greater specificity from Congress on the limits to executive discretion. The most important areas requiring greater specificity pertain to the sanctity of contracts and extraterritorial application of controls. Other proposals to add "hoops and hurdles" are either unworkable or unrealistic, since they impose formalistic steps easily fulfilled without adding more certainty or better analysis, and their procedures could be followed, without affecting the results at all.

Controls imposed on exports will hurt no matter what procedures are followed; in fact, that is the crux of the argument. It is a simple fact that the government controls exports. This is a "regulation" in a climate of deregulation, and any attempt to gloss over this fact minimizes the problem. If the hurt is accompanied by perceived unfairness, by international competitive disadvantage, or by an increasingly adversarial relationship with the government, then the hurt is translated into an urge to do something. On this, the business community seems united.

Foreign policy controls have been used relatively sparingly, have affected few industries, and have been imposed only in cases with congressional and allied support in almost every instance. The executive has not abused the delegation of administration from Congress, and the courts have not intervened to overturn the decisions of the administrators. In sum, the program has not been run badly. While debates may rage about the effectiveness of controls in achieving the objectives in target countries, there is no debate about the support for the presidential authority in this area, authority that must be preserved with as few limitations as possible. Indeed, foreign affairs are too volatile, change too fast, and are too fragile to be subject to the same constraints routinely placed on domestic political matters. It is clear that changes in the Export Administration Act can be made without undermining its basic structure, and that is what Congress should do.

NOTES

1. Export Administration Act, Section 3(2)(B), Section 3(7), and Section 3(8).

2. S/Rep. No. 96–169 Cong., 1st Sess., p. 3.

3. U.S. v. Brumage, District Court of New York 1974, 377 F. Supp. 144.

4. 47 FR 27250, June 24, 1982.

# 18

# NATIONAL SECURITY DIMENSIONS OF INTERNATIONAL TRADE

## W. Bruce Weinrod

This chapter addresses the national security ramifications of international trade policy. It addresses that very narrow and specific topic from the perspective of the maximum ideal approach, acknowledging that policymakers, in the give and take of everyday activities, will not necessarily be able to implement every recommendation. First a brief framework of analysis is useful to provide the background for the recommendations made in this chapter. Free trade is the ideal international economic system, yet the imperfections of the real world necessitate a system that does not reach that ideal. Still, the standard of free trade should be maintained and used to judge this country's actions on a day-to-day basis. National security concerns are perhaps the most important and inevitable limitation on the ideal of a free trade regimen, and in the contemporary world, this means that the United States must maintain an international trade policy that can respond to the Soviet challenge.

For most of the 1970s, the United States and its allies, under the influence of detente theories, did not place sufficient emphasis on the security aspects of international trade. This lax posture, combined with aggressive Soviet bloc efforts, substantially harmed Western security. No trade policy can totally prevent the leakage of militarily useful technology to the Soviets; however, much can be prevented, much can be substantially delayed, and--this is perhaps the most important point of all--the cost of Soviet

access can be made high. The Reagan administration's policies, it should be noted, are a substantial improvement on
the recent past. These efforts must continue, and the authority of the President to restrict trade for security purposes
must be maintained and even strengthened when necessary. The
Soviets, it is clear, have accrued great benefits and caused
serious harm to Western security by obtaining access to
Western technology.[1]


## APPROACHES TO THE PROBLEM

Any discussion of the strategic aspects of international trade should start with an assessment of the nature
of the security threat facing the United States, followed by
an assessment of the types of policies that, in general, are
most likely to be helpful or harmful to U.S. security.

First of all, to state the obvious--or what should be
obvious but is often only that when it is vividly spelled
out--the government of the Soviet Union is based on an ideological system that requires and justifies expansion and
seeks to undermine Western values and security interests
wherever and whenever the opportunity arises. To be sure,
this perception is not shared, even now, by all elite opinion
sectors in the United States or elsewhere in the West.

To oversimplify, there are two basic economic approaches
to dealing with the Soviet challenge. One calls for "normalization" of economic relations with the Soviet Union. Proponents of this approach contend that economic exchange will
do some, if not all, of the following: make the Soviets
more aware of the outside world, make them less ideological
and less repressive internally, reduce their expansionist
tendencies, and force them to shift resources from the military to the civilian sector. These people, therefore, are
very enthusiastic about increasing economic ties with the
Soviet Union.

Although these advocates of economic ties rarely support the transfer of purely military items that clearly and
directly benefit the Soviet military, they generally en-
dorse increased trade with the Soviets, relatively loose in-
terpretations of what is of military benefit to the Soviets,
and the offering of subsidized credit and official guaran-

tees. They favor loose restrictions on exchanges of information and a relatively unrestrictive allied export control posture that looks for a least-common-denominator approach among the allies rather than a strong leadership role for the United States in setting the standard for trading with the Soviets.

The other approach calls for great skepticism in economic relations with the Soviets. As an absolute minimum, proponents of this approach believe that technology transfer should be tightly restricted and that any doubt about the potential use of a technology for military purposes should be resolved in favor of restrictions on its export. They also believe that the United States must take the lead in making decisions to restrict technology.

These different perspectives continue today, and they will probably continue in the future, for there are some on both sides of the debate who will never be persuaded by evidence or experience. This debate is fascinating; the theoretical arguments on both sides are strong and persuasive. Fortunately, there is now evidence and experience that make it clear that one side, that which proclaimed great benefits to be gained from economic detente, was wrong, and the side that warned that such an approach would not produce the proclaimed results, and would indeed be harmful to Western security, was basically correct.

The advocates of economic detente were wrong on many points, but the scope of this book requires this chapter to focus on only one--the security dimension. First of all, Soviet defectors have said that the expanded U.S.-Soviet economic exchange during the 1970s did not lead the Soviets into normal commercial relationship with the West. Instead, the Soviets established a special group to obtain, by whatever means necessary, the advanced Western technology required for Soviet military efforts.

Second, the detente culture provided a justification for Western governments that wanted to indulge the private sector's interest in sales to the Soviet bloc, even where there were obvious security implications. For example, the Pullman Corporation assisted the Soviets in setting up production lines at the Kama River truck plant, and the Bryant Manufacturing Company sold equipment that facilitated the production of miniature ball bearings of great precision.

MINIMIZING NATIONAL SECURITY RAMIFICATIONS

These points lead to the main focus of this chapter, which is the question of what international trade policy will minimize harm to U.S. national security while taking into account the other legitimate and important objectives of U.S. international trade policy. A number of the suggestions made here have already been made by other people, and others are new.

For purposes of discussion, these policy recommendations are divided into those policies that are most related to the unilateral aspects of U.S. trade policy and those that are more associated with the multilateral concerns of security policy. These are not necessarily in order of importance.

## Improving Unilateral Aspects of Trade Control

The United States should follow several unilateral policies to ensure that the security of the Western world is adequately protected. Number one, it should rationalize the administrative responsibilities for the security aspects of international trade, ideally through the establishment of an Office of Strategic Trade, which would be an independent agency devoting continual high-level attention and sufficient resources to security questions. An unintended side benefit of the creation of this office could be the speeding of consideration of security issues and a narrower focus, both of which would benefit the private sector. Until this is accomplished, the creation of an Undersecretary of Commerce for Export Policy or a White House office to coordinate security dimensions of trade would be helpful.

Second, the United States should improve the effectiveness of the Department of Defense's role in licensing decisions. Given that the security dimension is the real reason for national security export controls, it simply makes sense for the Department of Defense to have the right to object to transfers to any nation, whether it be an ally or an enemy of the United States. Disagreements between the Commerce Department and Defense Department or other agencies should be resolved at higher levels, up to and including the President. The Department of Defense may be overzealous at times, but this is preferable to the situation that existed in the 1970s. An Office of Strategic Trade, however, would balance the concerns of the Department of Defense with other legitimate concerns.

Three, the United States should strengthen its enforcement capabilities. The Office of Export Administration of the Department of Commerce has not always performed effectively, certainly not as effectively as it could. There has been extraordinary progress in the past few years, but there are inherent institutional reasons for moving that criminal enforcement responsibility from the Commerce Department to the Customs Agency.

In addition to giving priority enforcement authority to the Customs Agency, a number of types of specific criminal enforcement authority should be given to the agency that has responsibility. The possession of restricted goods with intent to export them should be made illegal, sentences and fines for illegal diversion should be increased, court-authorized surveillance should be expressly permitted when there is probable cause that a violation of technology laws is being committed, and the controlled commodity list should be revised. Furthermore, the United States should negotiate with its allies for the prosecution or extradition of those believed to have violated U.S. export law and should make it a federal offense to steal, receive, buy, or bribe to obtain technology with the intent to export it unlawfully. In addition, the President should have the authority to restrict the transfer of items to U.S. diplomatic offices and other entities under the control of countries to which export controls have been applied.

Four, this country needs to maintain controls on trade with non-Soviet bloc nations. There is a surface appeal to the argument that U.S. controls on trade with its allies can be relaxed, and this should be a long-term policy goal. Unfortunately, at the present time this would be an unwise policy because Washington's allies have generally been much more relaxed than the United States in guarding against technology leakage. Some of that is certainly a result of U.S. policies in the early 1970s, which set a precedent and created an example for the Europeans to follow, but they have taken it to extremes. Also, eliminating controls on West-West

trade would send mixed signals at a time when great pressure
is being placed on the allies to tighten controls. Although
there are recent indications that the Reagan administration's
approach has produced a firmer attitude on the part of the
allies, the withdrawal of authority at the present time would
undercut whatever continuing pressures the United States
needs to put on its allies.

In addition, there are security-related items that the
President may judge should not be available even to allies.
There is, of course, also the fact that current controls
make the tracing of illegal diversions substantially easier.
Certainly, this is even more true with regard to trade with
neutral European nations such as Austria, Finland, Switzerland, and Sweden, which has accounted for much of the illegal diversion of technology to the Soviet bloc. The leverage there is very important; it has produced effects most
recently in Austria and also in Switzerland.

A fifth point is that the foreign availability test
should not be inordinately loosened. All things being equal,
of course, if the exact same item is available in quantity
elsewhere, it makes little sense for the United States to
restrict its export unilaterally. As Undersecretary of
Commerce Lional Olmer has pointed out, however, there may be
times when export restrictions are appropriate despite foreign availability. Certainly there are a number of very important questions about foreign availability and quantity
resupply that need to be examined. It would be a mistake to
take the case of the exporter at face value, as some people
have suggested. Rather, the burden of persuasion should be
on those making the case for foreign availability. The resources devoted to this issue certainly should be increased
and should receive priority, but the exporter's case should
not be presumed to be correct.

There are a number of difficult issues that have to be
resolved in determining foreign availability. The determination requires subjective evaluations of such matters as com-
parability (is the non-U.S. item really the same, or is it
only similar?), quantity (can the non-U.S. producer supply
quantities or resupply, especially in a relatively short
time, and is the quantity sufficient to be militarily significant?), quality (is the item likely to last as long or
be as efficient?), price (Soviet bloc hard-currency problems
make this relevant), and maintenance.

Six, Washington should establish a systematic early warning system. Two interrelated systems should be established, or at least be put in one place. One would monitor emerging U.S. technologies with a view toward alerting both the government and private sector if the technology has military applicability. The second system would monitor Soviet technology needs. The Soviets will deploy dozens of weapons systems in the next decade. By analyzing the technology that they are going to require for such systems—including missile guidance, computerized aircraft designs, and submarine and airborne navigation—the United States can prevent or at least limit some of the Soviet breakthroughs.

Another needed step is to increase the private sector's role in control efforts. The business community should participate in the national security export control process. It could help determine the items to be restricted and can assist with enforcement, including counterespionage efforts. The object of control is not to penalize the private sector but to enhance Western security.

Eight, the United States ought to tighten information flows. The Soviets have obtained a lot of information via academic activities. There is a need to find a balance between the usefulness of a free flow of ideas and the need to make sure that advanced technology is not unduly leaked through conferences and papers. There are several ways in which the United States can restrict this particular flow without impinging inordinately on the free flow of ideas between academics. It can classify information, restrict communication of technical data to foreign nationals, require prepublication review by the Defense Department for key government-financed research, establish voluntary agreements to limit flows of technical data, and limit access to the United States for certain foreign nationals.

The United States also should continue to maintain strict licensing standards. This is really the heart of the matter. Procedures are important, but the licensing decisions themselves are crucial and should err, if at all, on the side of security. U.S. technology, while increasingly being tested by that of other nations, is still in many cases the most advanced. Equally important, U.S. decisions and practices still set the standard for others. It should be remembered that technology that is relatively obsolete by U.S. standards may still be crucial to the Soviet bloc.

Ten, the President should have the authority to impose
import controls.  The security aspects of U.S. trade policy
currently focus exclusively on export controls.  There is no
good reason why the power to impose import controls should
not be added to the presidential arsenal.  Specifically, the
President should have the option of prohibiting imports from
an overseas subsidiary of a U.S. company that violates U.S.
law by reexporting U.S. items and from a non-U.S. company
outside the United States that violates U.S. or COCOM restrictions.  The awareness of this potential penalty will, at a
minimum, make potential violators think twice before ignoring controls, especially given the vast size of the U.S. market.

Eleven, the United States must assure the protection
of its technology when foreign companies obtain control of a
U.S. company that is high-technology-oriented.  While no
solution is available at the present, this matter must be
addressed soon.


Improving Multilateral Aspects
of Trade Control

Clearly, allied cooperation is very important to an
effective national security export policy, and the United
States must continue doing all that it can to improve cooperation.  But to believe that this can be done by statements
and requests without having some leverage totally ignores
the reality of the past few years.  The empirical evidence
clearly shows that it was only under continuing U.S. pressure
in the past year or two that significant changes have begun
to be made.

The West needs to continue to strengthen COCOM.  The
United States should substantially increase its funding to
establish an independent office with a large full-time staff
of experts, and it should increase high-level participation
with regularly scheduled ministerial-level meetings to give
policy guidance.  It needs to work for the establishment of
COCOM standards for evaluating license applications and cooperate in multilateral policing and common sanctions against
COCOM violators.  Most important, the defense ministries of
the allied nations should have a defined mandatory involve-

ment in each COCOM delegation. The United States should also work to establish a private-sector multilateral advisory committee to advise on emerging technologies.

Given continuing strong U.S. leadership, the implementation of these measures would help to ensure that the West is not seriously harmed via technology leakage. If the United States could be assured that the export control policies of other nations were serious rather than mere paper-stamping exercises, then some U.S. control policies could be reevaluated. One might note, parenthetically, that roughly half--depending on how one calculates it--of the U.S. defense budget is devoted to NATO-related matters. It is not too much to expect the allies to display a greater willingness to accommodate legitimate U.S. concerns in this area. To the extent that major economic sacrifices take place, consideration should be given to some way of distributing the economic burden of national security controls among the allies.

The next point is that the United States should maintain "extraterritorial authority." Current law gives the President authority to impose so-called extraterritorial controls when he feels they are necessary. Such controls are of two types: restrictions on exports of non-U.S.-made items by U.S. subsidiaries located abroad and controls on the reexport by non-U.S. companies located overseas of items originally exported from the United States. Such controls should be used sparingly, but they are essential not only to effective export controls but also to the effective enforcement of U.S. antiterrorism and antiboycott laws. Furthermore, the absence of such controls would be an incentive for U.S. businesses to move overseas.

Unfortunately, assertions of extraterritorial jurisdiction may occasionally increase political tensions with our allies. Certainly, allied reaction should be heavily weighed, but it cannot be a determining factor when important U.S. national security or foreign policy interests are at issue. Those who argued that the pipeline sanctions would have a severe, long-lasting impact on U.S.-European relations were wrong. Recently, French Defense Minister Charles Hernu stated that the disagreement "did not leave any scars" and "we do not even speak of it." In their June 1983 communiqué, the NATO foreign ministers agreed that "economic relations with [the Soviet bloc] must remain consistent with broad allied security concerns."

With respect to reexport controls, the Export Administration Act permits the President to require a foreign company to obtain a reexport license in order to export a specified item to another country. This means that the company has to receive approval from both its government and the United States. This provision should remain in force until U.S. allies more consistently take into account U.S. security concerns. Extraterritoriality is a means to an end. If and when other nations have secure safeguards and tough standards regarding technology diversion, there will be no real need for such action.

The question has been raised: by what authority does the United States impose extraterritorial restrictions? A short answer is that the U.S. Congress has, in fact, authorized extraterritoriality, and thus far no reports have said that this is something that cannot be done. In the legal sense, it is authorized and can be done. The real question is, at this point at least, whether it is a wise thing to do. The main concern there, of course, is the reaction of the allies. Again, the allies are certainly not pleased with such policies, but it has not become a major problem in U.S.-allied relations and was not even at the time of the pipeline decision. The fact is that the pipeline decision--which had some problems in terms of its timing and rationale, not in terms of what it tried to do--did not have any long-standing impact on NATO. In fact, the pipeline sanction led to major allied studies of energy dependency, technology transfer, and credit flows. The allies have disagreed on a wide variety of economic matters since the inception of the alliance and continue to disagree to this day on matters ranging from steel to agricultural products.

Finally, it should be noted that if every single suggestion made here were implemented, the institutional infrastructure for minimizing security problems emanating from international trade would be solid. Yet it is important to keep all of this in perspective.

Ultimately, an institutional structure is only as strong as the leadership at the top. If the President and his high-level policymakers do not place a high priority on the security aspects of trade, then no institutional structure can assure protection of U.S. security interests.

Important licensing decisions, as well as the degree of emphasis to be placed on enforcement activities and pressuring U.S. allies, are determined by the White House. If the President chooses to downplay security considerations, he can and will do so despite all of the institutional mechanisms in place.

## CONCLUSION

National security export controls are an important means of protecting U.S. interests. Some argue that crucial items will reach the Soviet bloc eventually anyway and that, therefore, tight controls are not warranted or useful. This argument ignores the principal benefit of controls, which is that they delay the absorption of new militarily relevant technology by the Soviet bloc. In the past, there was an eight- to ten-year technology acquisition gap from West to East, but that has already been reduced substantially, and in some instances the Soviet bloc is applying Western dual-use technology for military purposes even before the West does. Given the Soviet bloc conventional advantage in Europe and the increasing Western emphasis on new technologies to counter the large Soviet quantitative advantage, controls are even more necessary than before. Furthermore, each Soviet bloc technological breakthrough results in huge added costs to NATO nations for countermeasures.

On the broadest plane, both national security and foreign policy controls must be seen within the context of the overall East-West struggle. The looser export controls of the detente era did not, as predicted by its formulators, result in more responsible Soviet behavior. Instead, security-related exports were used to build up the Soviet bloc's military capability, and other trade was used to escape the consequences of disastrous economic policies.

Given current Soviet conduct, it should be the policy of the United States (and a consensus of Western nations) to restrict dual-use goods or technology and to give the President the option to limit trade for foreign policy reasons, such as the Soviet invasion of Afghanistan or the imposition of martial law in Poland.

Economic matters are an increasingly important aspect of overall relations among nations. The export policies of the United States therefore cannot be considered solely in the context of ordinary business concerns, important though these may be. The context must be broadened to include U.S. security and Soviet behavior. Under present conditions, the correct policy is to err, if at all, on the side of protecting Western security and granting the President foreign policy authority and flexibility.

NOTE

1. For background on technology transfer to the Soviet Union, see: Central Intelligence Agency, Soviet Acquisition of Western Technology (Washington, D.C.: Government Printing Office, 1982); U.S. Senate, Permanent Subcommittee on Investigations of the Governmental Affairs Committee, Transfer of United States High Technology to the Soviet Union and Soviet Bloc Nations, 97th Cong., 2d sess., November 15, 1982; U.S. Congress, Office of Technology Assessment, Technology and East-West Trade (Washington, D.C.: Government Printing Office, 1979) and Update, May 1983; Paige Bryan et al., "Capitalists and Commissars," Policy Review (Fall 1982), pp. 19-34; Miles Costick, "Strategic Trade, Economic Sanctions and the Security of the Free World," in Geoffrey Stewart-Smith, ed., Towards a Grand Strategy for Global Freedom (London: Foreign Affairs Research Institute, 1981).

# INDEX

# ABOUT THE EDITORS AND CONTRIBUTORS

MICHAEL R. CZINKOTA is Chairman of the National Center for
Export-Import Studies at Georgetown University, where he is
also a member of the faculty of Marketing and International
Business.  He studied law and business administration at the
University of Erlangen-Nuernberg in Germany and was a partner in an export-import firm.  In 1975, he won a Fulbright
Award and studied at The Ohio State University, where he re-
ceived his MBA in 1976 and his Ph.D. in 1980.
    Dr. Czinkota has written extensively on the subject of
international trade in publications such as Columbia Journal
of World Business and Journal of International Business
Studies.  His most recent publications are five books, entitled Export Policy, Export Management, Export Development
Strategies,  U.S. International Economic Policy 1981, and
U.S.-Latin American Trade Relations.

DON BONKER is a United States Congressman, Third District,
Washington.

WILLIAM E. BROCK is the United States Trade Representative.

DAVID H. BUSWELL is Director of Government Affairs, Fiatallis
North America, Inc.

MILES M. COSTICK is President, Institute on Strategic Trade.

JOHN F. DEALY is Distinguished Professor, School of Business
Administration, Georgetown University.

THOMAS B. EVANS, JR., is a partner in the law firm of
O'Connor & Hannan.

PAUL FREEDENBERG is an International Finance Economist for
the Senate Banking subcommittee on International Finance and
Monetary Affairs.

JOHN HEINZ is a United States Senator from Pennsylvania.

GARY CLYDE HUFBAUER is a Senior Fellow at the Institute for International Economics.

KEMPTON B. JENKINS is Vice President for Government Affairs, ARMCO, Inc.

RICHARD F. KAUFMAN is Assistant Director and General Counsel for the Joint Economic Committee of Congress.

NEIL C. LIVINGSTONE is Senior Vice President, Gray & Company.

SCOT MARCIEL is Editor, National Center for Export-Import Studies, Georgetown University.

STANLEY D. NOLLEN IS A Fellow at the National Center for Export-Import Studies and Associate Professor at Georgetown University.

LIONEL OLMER is Undersecretary of Commerce for International Trade.

JOSEPH E. PATTISON is a partner in the law firm of O'Connor & Hannan.

LEONARD SANTOS is International Trade Counsel at the Senate Finance Committee.

JEFFREY J. SCHOTT is Visiting Fellow at the Institute for International Economics and is associated with the Diebold Institute for Public Policy Studies in New York.

RAYMOND J. WALDMANN is President and Director of Global U.S.A., Inc.

W. BRUCE WEINROD is Director of Foreign Policy and Defense Studies at The Heritage Foundation.